Walking Rh...

40 Hikes for Nature and History Lovers

with Pictures, GPS Coordinates, and Trail Maps

John Kostrzewa prepares to climb the rocky steps of the "cathedral," a natural cleft cut between high rock walls on the trail through Long Pond Woods Wildlife Refuge in Hopkinton.

Walking Rhode Island

40 Hikes for Nature and History Lovers with Pictures, GPS Coordinates, and Trail Maps

John Kostrzewa

Walking Rhode Island: 40 Hikes for Nature and History Lovers with Pictures, GPS Coordinates, and Trail Maps
Copyright © 2023 John Kostrzewa

Produced and printed by Stillwater River Publications.

All rights reserved. Written and produced in the United States of America. This book may not be reproduced or sold in any form without the expressed, written permission of the author(s) and publisher.

Visit our website at **www.StillwaterPress.com** for more information.

First Stillwater River Publications Edition

ISBN: 978-1-960505-46-0

Library of Congress Control Number: 2023910729

1 2 3 4 5 6 7 8 9 10
Written by John Kostrzewa.
Cover photo by John Kostrzewa. The Wood River flows south under the Appalachian Mountain Club Bridge along the Mount Tom Trail in the Arcadia Management Area. Most photographs are by John Kostrzewa. Some pictures were taken by fellow hikers or others Kostrzewa met on the trails.
Cover & interior book design by Matthew St. Jean.
Published by Stillwater River Publications, Pawtucket, RI, USA.

Stillwater River Publications and the author assume no liability for accidents happening to, or injuries sustained by, readers who engage in activities described in this book.

   Names: Kostrzewa, John, author.
   Title: Walking Rhode Island : 40 hikes for nature and history lovers / John
      Kostrzewa.
   Description: First Stillwater River Publications edition. | Pawtucket, RI, USA :
      Stillwater River
   Publications, [2023]
   Identifiers: ISBN: 978-1-960505-46-0 (paperback) | LCCN: 2023910729
   Subjects: LCSH: Hiking—Rhode Island—Guidebooks. | Trails—Rhode Island—
      Guidebooks. | Rhode Island—History. | LCGFT: Guidebooks.
   Classification: LCC: GV199.42.R4 K67 2023 | DDC: 796.5109745—dc23

The views and opinions expressed in this book are solely those of the author(s) and do not necessarily reflect the views and opinions of the publisher.

For Carol, Stephen, Andrew, and Daniel.

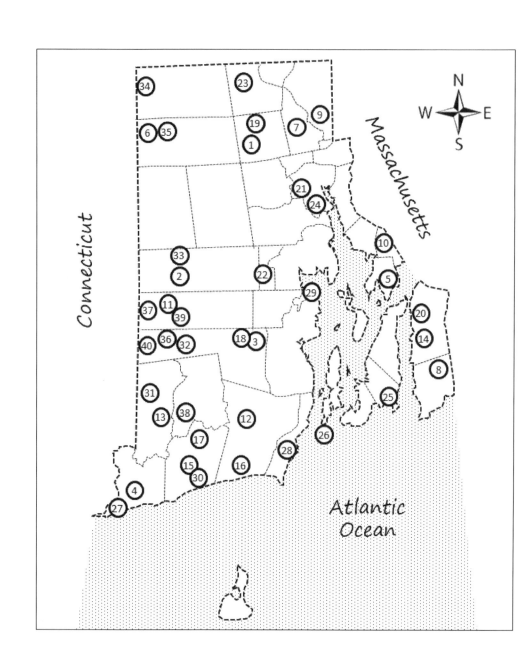

Contents

Acknowledgements ix
Introduction xi
How to Use This Book xv

Family Walks

1 Ken Weber Conservation Area 1
2 Maxwell Mays Wildlife Refuge 7
3 Cuttyhunk Brook Preserve 12
4 John C. Champlin Glacier Park 19
5 Mount Hope Farm 24
6 Hawkins Pond 31
7 Moshassuck River Preserve 35
8 Simmons Mill Pond Management Area 41
9 The Monastery 45
10 Haile Farm Preserve 51

Nature Walks

11 Tillinghast Pond Management Area 59
12 Great Swamp 64
13 Black Farm 70
14 Weetamoo Woods/Pardon Gray 77
15 Vin Gormley Trail 81
16 Trustom Pond 87
17 Francis C. Carter Memorial Preserve 93
18 Fisherville Brook Wildlife Refuge 99
19 Wolf Hill Forest Preserve 105
20 Fort Barton Woods 111

Urban Walks

21 Neutaconkanut Hill 119
22 West Warwick Greenway 123
23 Slatersville 129
24 Roger Williams Park 137

Coastal Hikes

25	Sachuest Point National Wildlife Refuge	143
26	Beavertail State Park	149
27	Napatree Point	155
28	Black Point	161
29	Goddard Memorial State Park	167
30	Ninigret National Wildlife Refuge	172

Challenging Hikes

31	Long Pond Woods	181
32	Mount Tom Trail	187
33	Parker Woodland Wildlife Refuge	193
34	Tri-Town Marker / Buck Hill Management Area	199
35	Walkabout Trail / George Washington Management Area	205
36	Escoheag Trail / Ben Utter Trail / Stepstone Falls	209
37	Pine Top	217
38	Carolina Management Area	223
39	Wickaboxet Management Area	229
40	Pachaug Trail	233

Trail Tips	*239*
More "Walking Rhode Island" Columns	*243*

Acknowledgements

Hiking is more fun with friends. So is publishing a book.

I've been fortunate to have many former colleagues, family members and friends who helped me with *Walking Rhode Island*.

Gary Zebrun, a former assistant managing editor/news at The Providence Journal, offered advice and encouragement from the first time I mentioned the idea of compiling my newspaper columns into a book. Zebrun, the author of three novels, reviewed and edited the columns, wrote fresh headlines and helped organize the material.

Michael Delaney, a former managing editor/visuals at The Journal, helped choose the pictures for the book and suggested concepts for the front cover, inside pages, and back cover.

Jeff Walker, a hiker, trail runner and a board member of the Westerly Land Trust, created the trail maps, checked the accuracy of my work and became a friend during the project.

Kathleen Hill, Sunday news editor and arts editor at The Journal, edited the columns before they appeared in the newspaper and online, wrote the headlines and worked hard to create the best possible presentation.

Over the years, many friends have hiked with me. Among those who accompanied me on the 40 trails in the book are John Caramadre, Rick DeGrandpre, George Robillard, Jim Robinson and my brother, Peter Kostrzewa.

I relied on many other hikers and their trail reports. I owe a special debt of gratitude to Ken Weber, the late outdoorsman, environmentalist and nature columnist for The Journal, who wrote several books that I often consulted before heading out on the trails. I also appreciated the readers who offered advice and the experts at Rhode Island's state agencies and nonprofit conservation organizations who answered my questions about what I found on my hikes.

My three sons, Stephen, Andrew and Daniel, listened to all my stories about hiking, offered suggestions and joked with me about interesting aspects of the walks. Stephen, a writer and editor, edited the first drafts of all my "Walking Rhode Island" columns.

My wife, Carol, encouraged my hiking and looked over each of my columns before they were published. For the last 42 years, she has read, edited and improved every substantive story or column I've written.

Thank you to all.

Introduction

Writing a hiking column, or publishing a book, never crossed my mind when I retired from The Providence Journal.

I had worked 42 years in the newspaper industry, including the last 29 at The Journal as a reporter, assistant business editor, business editor, columnist and assistant managing editor who helped run the newsroom.

I loved the work, but, like so many journalists these days, I took a buyout. I was exhausted.

When I left the newsroom for the last time, I had no idea if I would ever work again.

Since then, I've learned that when one career ends, another can start. I found out it's possible to try new things with the help of family, friends and former colleagues.

And I came to understand that when you have retired, been laid off, or furloughed, you still have more to contribute. You just have to give it some time to find your new path.

When I walked away from The Journal in May 2017, I set some simple goals: get healthier; work on our long-neglected house; reconnect with family and friends; and try to figure out what comes next.

I started by climbing a ladder to paint our house. I'm no handyman, but I enjoyed the work outdoors that seemed so different than sitting at a desk and editing reporters' stories.

I also decided to walk for exercise and explore Rhode Island. I joined a group of friends from the days when our boys had participated in the Scouting program and we had been adult leaders.

Our first hikes took us around Yawgoog Pond in Rockville and through the Arcadia Management Area, the 14,000-acre state preserve in South County.

During seven weekends, we walked the North South Trail, which runs for 78 miles from Charlestown's beaches to the state border in Burrillville. I realized I had spent most of my life in Rhode Island in the Greater Providence area and knew little about other interesting and beautiful parts of the state.

I researched the history and terrain of the trails and posted my reports on social media. I was surprised by how many people seemed to like them and I reconnected with friends, relatives and former coworkers.

As I got stronger, our group ventured into the White Mountains of New Hampshire and climbed some of the 4,000 foot peaks. We capped the summer by traveling to Baxter State Park in Maine and crossed the Knife Edge, a narrow, rocky ledge that leads to the 5,267-foot peak of Mt. Katahdin.

It felt rewarding.

As the summer ended, I started to worry about what I would do when the weather turned colder. I also realized that for the first time since I was a teenager, I didn't have a job to go to after Labor Day.

I was hiking on the Franconia Ridge in New Hampshire when my cell phone rang unexpectedly with a call from Bryant University. The administrators were trying to fill a last-minute vacancy to teach a class called Writing Workshop. My name came up.

I had never taught college students, but I took the job to give it a try.

Two weeks later, after scrambling to put together a syllabus with the help of some Journal colleagues who were also at Bryant, I walked into a classroom of 20 first-year students and started to teach.

I loved it.

Between classes, I continued to hike in state management areas and other properties managed by local land trusts and nonprofit conservation organizations across the state. I benefited from the physical activity, and, as I walked, I planned lessons and thought about the students and how to be a better teacher. I enjoyed the quiet time to think.

I taught for three years until COVID-19 struck and, for several reasons, I decided not to return to Bryant in the summer of 2020.

Again, I wondered what, if anything, comes next. I continued to hike, mostly by myself during the pandemic, and thought about how I could contribute during the public health and economic crisis.

I wrote some freelance stories for The Journal about the effects of COVID-19 on business and the economy. Readers and former colleagues encouraged me to keep writing.

As the virus seemed to get worse, I decided to write more, but I also thought there may be some value in sharing what I learned from my hikes.

INTRODUCTION

I noticed that more people and their children, who had been cooped up at home to work or study, were spending more time outdoors. Whenever I looked outside our house, I saw people walking through our neighborhood.

When I went on hikes, I was surprised by how many first-time hikers were on the trails and looking for ideas about where to go and what to take to stay safe.

I spoke with the editors at The Journal and pitched the idea of writing a hiking column. The goals were simple: take readers to places where they hadn't been. If they had been there, show them something new, including the history of the area, and share my thoughts about the nature, wildlife and geology that I see.

The editors suggested that I give it a try for a few weeks and I published my first column, "Walking Rhode Island," in January 2021. The columns appeared in the Sunday Providence Journal, on providencejournal.com and my Facebook page.

Readers wrote to me with questions, comments, criticisms, ideas and places to hike. I enjoyed their comments, the exercise, exploring Rhode Island, the research and the writing.

Since I started, I have now written more than 100 columns.

Some readers suggested that I compile the hikes into a book and the result is *Walking Rhode Island: 40 Hikes for Nature and History Lovers*.

They say there are no second acts in life. But I've had several since I left The Journal.

I plan to continue to hike and write the column, until somebody tells me to stop.

I hope you enjoy the book. Please let me know what you think and where you've been hiking.

Stay safe and I'll see you on the trail.

John Kostrzewa welcomes email at johnekostrzewa@gmail.com.

How to Use This Book

Walking Rhode Island is organized into five sections:

Family Walks are mostly flat, easy-to-follow paths that are perfect for parents, grandparents and guardians to explain the history of an area and point out trees, geological features and wildlife.

Nature Walks tend to be of easy or moderate difficulty and are a little longer than family walks. Sometimes the trails cover rocky terrain, cross brooks and traverse deep forests.

Coastal Walks offer views of the ocean or the bay. The trails are easy to moderate in difficulty and can take uneven routes over ledges and along cliffs.

Urban Walks follow sidewalks, bike paths or hard-packed trails. They are good for walkers who want to avoid insects in the woods during the summer. In winter, the black asphalt walkways dry quickly in the sun and can be a safer walk than on other trails.

Challenging Hikes are the longest and most strenuous. Because the trails are sometimes not well marked or confusing, these walks take extra planning and care. Build up your strength and trail savvy on the easier hikes before you work up to more challenging ones.

Many of the trails can fall into more than one category. For example, some of the nature walks can be family walks, too.

Reading the description of a hike will help you pick a walk and provide a full picture of it, including historical landmarks, wildlife, vegetation and geological features.

Each description has an estimate of the difficulty - easy, moderate or challenging. But remember, difficulty is subjective based on a hiker's ability, strength, skill and experience.

Also, there's an approximate distance and estimated walking time. Each walker's pace is different, though, so use the information as a guideline, not gospel.

In addition to taking you through the hikes, I've included some basic details such as the GPS coordinates of the trailhead, how to get there, whether there is a parking lot, if dogs are allowed and when I last hiked the trail. The date of the hike is important because trails change in different seasons. A path that is bone dry in summer could be flooded in the spring and covered with ice in the winter.

Before you head out, check out some current, online trail reports that are posted by other hikers or the organization that manages the property. Search online by the name of the trail or the preserve where you are hiking.

The 40 hikes in *Walking Rhode Island* are spread across 24 cities and towns in the state and are numbered on the Contents page. To get a general idea of where the trail is located, find the number of the trail you are interested in on the state map.

When you plan your hike, study the map and photos included with each walk. Familiarize yourself with the pictures so you can recognize the features.

The maps include parking areas, landmarks, waterways, bridges, churches, cemeteries, marshes and the distances between points to help you visualize the trail and estimate how far you've hiked or how far you still need to go.

In some cases, the distance you walk won't exactly match the distance in the trail description or on the map. That's because I sometimes took side trails or left the trail briefly to explore a historic site or other landmark.

The maps use arrows to show the direction of the hike and include whether the trails are loops that return to the trailhead. Some routes require placing a car at the end of the trail or backtracking to the start.

After you study the map, take a cell phone picture to carry with you.

As you prepare to hike, consult the Trail Tips section at the back of the book for ideas about what to take with you, how to follow trail marks and how to stay safe.

All the information in the book, including the maps, has been reviewed to make the guide as accurate and useful as possible.

But trails can change over time. Sometimes they are closed or rerouted to protect sensitive vegetation or to curb erosion. New easements are secured that alter the paths and boundaries. Roads and properties can be renamed, as ownership of areas changes hands.

One last note:

Hikers have always helped each other to enjoy the best, safest experience on the trails. If you are out hiking and notice any changes from what's in the book, please send the information to johnekostrzewa@gmail.com

I'll do my best to share the information with other hikers.

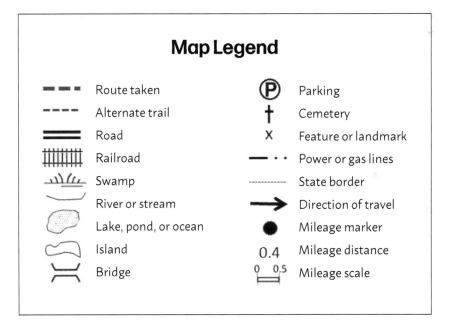

Family Walks

Cascade Brook tumbles over a 15-foot ledge in the Ken Weber Conservation Area.

A five-foot brick chimney stands on a 10-foot square foundation in an old campsite, shrine and recreation area.

1   Ken Weber Conservation Area

In the footsteps of outdoorsman Ken Weber, who wrote the RI hiking "bible"

Distance: 1.2 miles
Time: 90 minutes
Difficulty: Easy, but moderate over some ledges and rocky hillsides

Access: Drive west on Route 44 and turn right on Mapleville Road (also the entrance of The Village at Waterman Lake). Drive to the end of the road.
Parking: Available for a few cars at the trailhead
Dogs: Allowed, but must be leashed
Last Date Hiked: April 2023
Trailhead GPS: 41.87983, -71.56963

SMITHFIELD—Ken Weber, the late outdoorsman, environmentalist, and nature columnist for The Providence Journal, cut the trail here that's named in his honor.

The short, simple path along Cascade Brook fits Weber's view that hiking should not be a race through the woods but a chance to pause along the way, explore and think. "I don't consider walking a competitive sport or endurance event," he wrote in *Walks and Rambles in Rhode Island*, one of several guides he authored. Many consider the book the bible of hiking in the state.

"Those who plunge ahead—never stopping, looking neither left nor right—miss far too much. There is so much beauty, history, and wildlife along these routes that it would be a shame not to see as much as possible, and that takes a little slowing down," Weber wrote.

With his wife, Bettie, he planned, laid out and maintained the Ken Weber Conservation Area at Cascade Brook, which starts at the end of a short, dead-end road off Putnam Pike.

I set out from the trailhead, noted the map with Weber's picture at an information board and followed a blue-blazed path, once called Pig Run, for a few steps before the path turned right and through a stone wall. The trail follows some hard-packed dirt and a ledge before quickly reaching

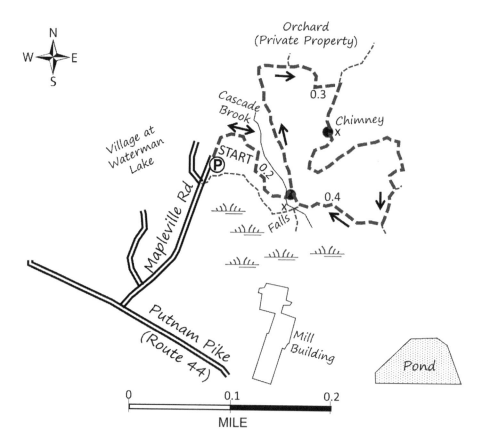

a colorful box stuffed with hand-written testimonials from young hikers. "My favorite place," wrote Robbie. The trail also passes a boulder with a neat sign:

Out of crowded dins
On ancient pathways into
Freshets of whispers

The path from there meanders under oaks, beaches and maples before reaching a small clearing. Cascade Brook flows slowly from the northwest on the flat, forest floor before tumbling down a 15-foot ledge. The better views of the small waterfall are from below and come later in the hike.

I followed the blue-blazed trail up a hillside, along the base of a huge rock outcropping and by some stone walls. The path may have been an old farm lane, as it loops along the perimeter of the 27-acre preserve and under pine trees and over soft needles.

Taking a side trail, I walked to the top of the hill and found an orchard with dozens of mature and newly planted fruit trees. There are new fence posts on the edge of the land that keep hikers from wandering onto the private property to pick apples.

Returning to the main path, I walked downhill around boulders and over ledges and found a curiosity—a 5-foot brick chimney standing on a 10-foot square concrete foundation. The base of the unusual chimney had four fireplaces, one on each side.

There are also the remains of cement posts on the ledges and a small rectangular structure made of cement.

One clue to their origins is a date etched in the foundation: May 4, 1942.

I learned later that the structure was part of a campsite, recreation area and shrine built by youngsters who lived at St. Aloysius Home about three-quarters of a mile away, according to the Smithfield Historical Society. The orphanage, home to up to 224 children, was owned and run by the Catholic Diocese of Providence and had a Boy Scout Troop.

At one time, the site also had an altar, table, and grotto with a religious statue, and it was used for years for picnics. Little remains, except for the chimney and posts.

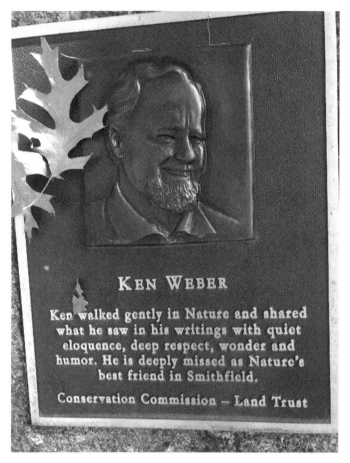

Ken Weber, the late naturalist, environmentalist and conservationist, is honored with a plaque at the Conservation Commission Center in Smithfield.

I sat there for a few minutes on a ledge on the overgrown site and tried to picture what it must have looked like 75 years ago, with all the kids enjoying the outdoors. Weber must have known the history and planned the trail to pass through the site.

When I decided it was time to move on, I got back on the trail and followed the blue blazes that circled the boundaries of the public property.

After crossing a stone wall, the path edges a marshy area and the Stillwater River to the south. There's a glimpse of some old textile mills that date to the 1800s and later became the Greenville Finishing Company. They are now antiques shops and small businesses.

The trail loops back along Cascade Brook and to the base of the waterfall I had seen from above.

After a recent rainstorm, there was a gush of falling water that filled a shallow pool below in a rocky bowl. Water also seeped in streams out of the ledges.

When I've been there after a long dry spell, water only trickles over the deep-green, mossy ledges in a thin horsetail of water. In the winter, I've marveled at 10-foot icicles sparkling in the sun and dripping into the icy stream below.

It's a place to pause and ponder, as Weber would have recommended.

I climbed a short, steep grade to the right of the waterfall, crossed Cascade Brook and took the trail back to where I started.

When Weber cut the trail, he was working at The Journal and writing his Saturday morning column about his nature walks. I remember him as a good editor who came from Ohio and liked to talk baseball. He was generous with his time, and when I asked, he offered hiking tips and recommendations about places to go.

I once asked him to lead a group of Scouts along the Mount Tom Trail in the Arcadia Management Area, and as we walked, he pointed out sights that we would never have noticed, such as two warring armies of ants marching toward each other.

When I asked a trail manager at Fort Nature Preserve in Smithfield about the benches on the banks of a pond, he recalled that during his rounds of the refuge, he often saw Weber patiently sitting there at dusk, waiting for the beavers to pop up. I still meet hikers on trails who mention Weber. He died in 2007.

Weber also was an active member of the Audubon Society and the Conservation Commission in Smithfield, where he lived. There's another trail he cut that's named for him in the town's Wolf Hill Forest Preserve.

At the base of the Wolf Hill trails, alongside Stump Pond and just outside the conservation center, there's a bronze plaque dedicated to Weber and his 30 years of public service promoting hiking in Rhode Island.

The inscription reads: "Ken walked gently in nature and shared what he saw in his writings with quiet eloquence, deep respect, wonder and humor."

That's quite a legacy.

Several streams feed Carr Pond, the centerpiece of the 295-acre Maxwell Mays Wildlife Refuge in Coventry.

2   Maxwell Mays Wildlife Refuge

"I would like this land to breathe." —*Artist Maxwell Mays*

Distance: 4 miles
Time: 2 hours
Difficulty: Easy to moderate with flat paths, some ridges and wetlands

Access: Take Exit 13B off I-95 and drive north on Route 102 for five miles to the trailhead on the right.
Parking: Available at the trailhead
Dogs: Not allowed
Last Date Hiked: January 2021
Trailhead GPS: 41.67077, -71.69434

COVENTRY—Maxwell Mays lived and hiked on this land for 60 years.

He also converted an old farmhouse in the 1940s into a residence and art studio, where he did some of his best painting of historic scenes in Rhode Island.

It's easy to understand the inspiration Mays took from walking the land.

There are icy streams feeding a partially frozen pond, a historic graveyard, a hilltop scattered with glacial boulders and the remains of a sheep and cattle farm on rolling ridges.

The landscape is quiet and beautiful on a clear, crisp early morning.

I set out with temperatures in the upper 30s from the trailhead and walked a perimeter path around a frost-covered meadow that sparkled in the sun. Mays ran his pony, Cindy, in the pasture. The trail led to a larger hayfield with a center-chimney house, behind the tree line to the south, where Mays worked and lived with several cats.

I followed the white-blazed trail markers around the fields and into the woods. In the early 1700s, Benjamin Carr began to work the land here and his family farmed the property for 200 years.

The trail crosses a dirt road and narrows through a thick hardwood forest. Just ahead on the right is the partially overground, stone-wall-lined

Maxwell Mays Wildlife Refuge

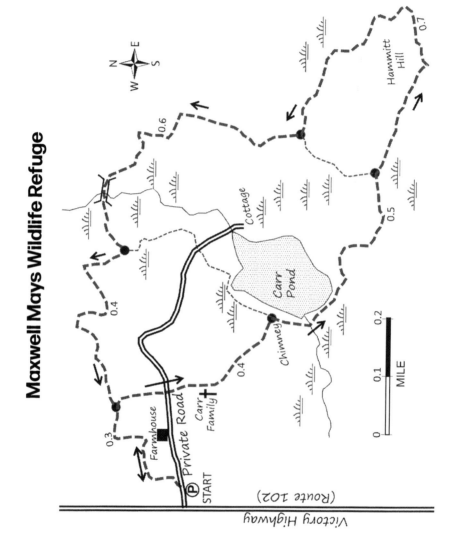

Carr family cemetery. When friends visited, Mays jokingly described the graveyard as the "used Carr lot."

After inspecting the headstones, I returned to the trail and walked under tall pines to the 11-acre Carr Pond, covered with a sheen of ice. There's a decaying stone chimney, repaired with bricks stamped S&H, for the Stiles and Hart Brick Co. founded in Bridgewater, Massachusetts, in 1886. The structure once attached to the hearth is long gone.

At the fireplace, hikers have two options. They can turn left and north on a white-blazed, 1.3-mile loop that runs uphill and then down and back to the meadow. There are some wetlands and flooding from beaver activity at the edge of the pond, but it's passable in most seasons.

I was more ambitious and turned right, south and then east, on the two-mile, yellow-blazed trail, with the pond on my left. Two plank bridges were submerged under swollen streams that empty into the pond.

I walked upstream about 40 yards to find a place to rock-hop across the water. I skirted the edge of the pond into an oak and beech forest. A gate blocks a road that leads to a private, secluded cabin on the north side of the pond. When Mays joined the Air Force during World War II, his father, W. Clarke S. Mays Sr., inventor of the metal pen clip and founder of the Mays Manufacturing Co., was exploring the woods one day and found the damaged wood and fieldstone camp. He made repairs before his son returned.

The trail continues east and crosses a blue-blazed cutoff trail that shortens the loop around the pond. But I stayed on the yellow-blazed trail and climbed 609-foot Hammitt Hill, the high point of the property. The hillside was covered with huge boulders, called glacial erratics and left from the Ice Age. One, nicknamed "smoking frog," has a wide, horizontal crack that was decorated with a log for a cigar and two small stones for eyes.

On the other side of the hill and along the trail are piles of stones that farmers cleared from the fields. I crossed a narrow, stone-slab bridge over a brook that runs from the pond to Quidnick Reservoir. Upstream, I inspected an earthen dam that may have been built to create a farm pond. Walking up the ridge, I explored stone walls, cellar holes and animal pens for cattle and sheep. The Carr family sold yarn and homespun cloth to settlers in the area.

The artist Maxwell Mays converted a farmhouse into a residence and art studio in the 1940s.

A decaying stone-and-brick chimney on the shores of Carr Pond may have once been part of a cabin or shelter.

Gnawed trees on the banks of Carr Pond are signs of beaver activity, which sometimes floods the trails.

At the top of the next rise, hikers can turn left and south to return on the white trail to the chimney on the banks of the pond. I turned right, hiked through a mountain laurel thicket and followed the trail back to the pasture where I'd started.

During my hike, I found the trails are mostly flat, well-marked and easy. But there are some moderate climbs up ridges, and hikers need to be careful crossing the flooded wetlands.

Maxwell Mays, who bought the property in 1941 from Mary Carr, a descendant of Benjamin Carr, moved into the renovated farmhouse and studio after his war service. His paintings of Rhode Island scenes became widely known.

When he died in 2009 at the age of 91, he bequeathed the buildings and 295 acres to the Audubon Society of Rhode Island, which maintains the Maxwell Mays Wildlife Refuge.

As he neared the end of his life, Mays, an artist, philanthropist, conservationist and storyteller, often told friends that the land he loved should stay in its natural state.

"I would like this land to breathe," he remarked, "because this has been very good to me and for me."

Well said, and thanks, Max.

3 Cuttyhunk Brook Preserve

Where smallpox victims were quarantined on a small farm in the 1800s

Distance: 2.5 miles
Time: 2 hours
Difficulty: Easy to moderate on some small ridges

Access: From Route 4, take Route 102 west to Sunderland Road on the right. The marked preserve is on the right.
Parking: Several spots at the trailhead
Dogs: Allowed, but must be leashed
Last Date Hiked: February 2022
Trailhead GPS: 41.58424, -71.55489

EXETER—A peaceful hike along the snow-covered paths in the Cuttyhunk Brook Preserve provided a respite from a harsh winter of blizzards, ice storms and frigid temperatures.

But I also found much more on my walk.

Just off the trail, on a hillock under a canopy of pine trees, is a smallpox cemetery with only one inscribed gravestone, bearing the name of Sarah Clarke Fenner.

There's no record of how she died, but historians point out that the date of her death fits with one of the peaks of the epidemic and that others buried nearby in unmarked graves succumbed to smallpox. Also, a short, wooded trail leads from the graveyard to stone foundations for several farm buildings where smallpox victims were once quarantined.

All of those findings gave me plenty to ponder, especially during the COVID-19 crisis, while taking a quiet, solo, winter walk in the woods.

I found the graveyard and historic foundations while following a loop trail in an 890-acre preserve managed by The Nature Conservancy, a nonprofit environmental organization.

From the trailhead, I followed a yellow-blazed path north through a thick forest of young, bright-green pine trees. The snow was about a foot deep, but previous hikers had broken the trail, so walking was not hard,

Cuttyhunk Brook flows under a stone bridge and southeast to the Queen River.

except for some slippery exposed rocks. The trail bent for a third of a mile down a long, gentle slope that once may have been a logging road. Some side paths, called skid trails, branched off the main route.

The path then crossed a stone bridge over the icy and narrow Cuttyhunk Brook. The water gurgles over stones in a shallow streambed and meanders southeast to the Queen River, which forms the eastern boundary of the preserve and is named for Quaiapan, a leader of the Narragansetts.

The derivation of the Cuttyhunk name is unclear. Other brooks in the area, such as Dutemple and Locke, are named for early settlers. But there's no record of a Cuttyhunk family living nearby. Some suggest that Cuttyhunk is a Native American term for "stream."

After the brook, the trail climbs and splits. I took the left branch that rose under oak trees, white pine trees, beech and a few black birches along a ridgeline that followed the course of the brook below. At times, stone walls crossed and lined the path, indicating this may have once been farmland. They were often built to mark property lines and pastureland, pen in animals or keep livestock from wandering into wetlands.

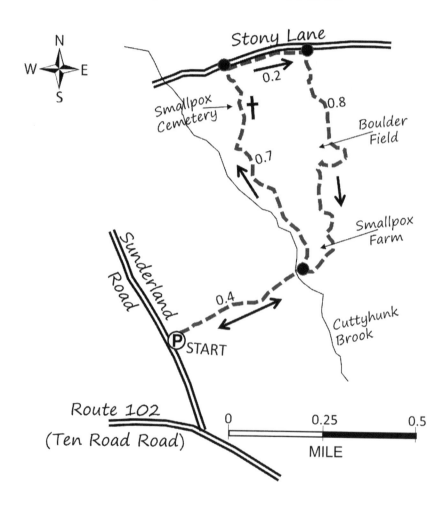

The well-blazed trail continued on, passing a small cemetery, marked with a sign, Rhode Island Historical Cemetery 149. I read the only inscribed white limestone headstone:

In memory of Sarah
Wife of Nathaniel Fenner
Daughter of Simon Clarke of Newport
Died Dec. 9, 1854 in her 72nd year.

While Fenner has a large, carved headstone, I found no public history of who Fenner was. The graves of others buried there have no markings and their names are lost to history.

A side trail on the right of the cemetery leads to the historic foundations.

But there was no path broken in the snow, and I continued north on the loop trail. The only sound was my boots crunching the snow or an occasional bird call deep in the woods. After about a half mile, the trail exited on Stony Lane, an unimproved town road.

The yellow blazes turned right on the hard-packed road, and on the left was a metal gate across a wide driveway, with signs marking private property of the Rhode Island Raccoon Hunters Association, a nonprofit hunting and fishing organization. The driveway and road were unplowed.

The Nature Conservancy also owns property to the north, but there are no public trails in that area.

I followed the road for a few hundred yards and reentered the woods on the blazed trail on the right. The path starts flat and then follows a ridgeline under tall pines with a low valley below on the right. Just ahead on the highest ground in the preserve (300 feet above sea level) was a long line of glacial erratics in a boulder field left from the Ice Age. They looked like snow-capped sentinels. When I hiked here before in drier weather, I recalled the deep-green coloration from the moss and lichen on the huge, gray rocks.

The trail continued through some downed trees recently cut and cleared from the path. I heard a gunshot to the south and remembered it's hunting season. Only archery hunting is allowed in the preserve. (State law requires wearing 200 square inches of blaze orange for safety.)

The preserve's smallpox cemetery has only one engraved headstone, for Sarah Clarke Fenner, who died in 1854.

After a downslope, the trail passed through some dense forest, wetlands and a small tributary that runs to the Queen River. The Nature Conservancy maintains as much forest canopy as possible in the Queen River watershed to protect water quality, keep the water temperatures cold and recharge the groundwater with natural flows from small streams.

Just ahead and on the right are the stone walls, foundations and cellar holes that may have once supported a large barn, storehouse and farmhouse.

I explored the remains and then rested on a split-log bench at an opening in the well-built stone walls. Before my hike, I had read a history of the area and the smallpox farm that was written in 2016 by Gary Boden, the late vice president of the Exeter Historical Association. I thought about his findings that smallpox victims in Exeter were quarantined in the stone structures. Those isolated worked on the farm to pay for their keep. Some died.

Boden found the earliest mention of a "Small Pox Place" in a 1849 deed for 30 acres owned by Beriah H. Lawton. The land later changed hands several times before being acquired in 2001 by The Nature Conservancy.

Other historians report that smallpox had swept over the state in several waves over the centuries and during Colonial times had decimated the early settlers and Native Americans who lived here.

In the mid-1800s, thousands more died, and state and town leaders fought the infectious disease by closing ports, appropriating money for smallpox hospitals and quarantining those infected on isolated farms. Several states mandated new vaccinations, including one called the "cow pox method" that some shunned and ridiculed as causing the growth of hooves and horns.

The outbreak in Exeter, and other cities and towns, seemed to have been especially severe from about 1840 to 1880. Town meeting records show payment for services for smallpox cases. Fenner's death in 1854 fits that timeframe.

Smallpox cases continued for years, and it wasn't until 1979 that the stubborn virus was declared globally eradicated, leaving a sparse history of those who died and were buried in unmarked graves.

Sitting on the land where smallpox victims had once lived, I thought about the quiet beauty along the trails that I had seen on a serene, cold winter day. But I also remembered the troubling history buried under the snow.

As the air got chilly, it was time to move on. I walked down a slope, recrossed Cuttyhunk Brook and retraced my steps to the trailhead.

I was tired from trudging through the snow but paused before leaving to look back into the silent, white sanctuary. During the two-hour hike, I hadn't seen another soul.

The view from Charlie's Overlook in the John C. Champlin Glacier Park in Westerly includes Winnapaug Pond, Misquammicut Beach, and Block Island Sound.

4   John C. Champlin Glacier Park

On land the Ice Age shaped

Distance: 3 miles
Time: 90 minutes
Difficulty: Easy, with some hills

Access: There are two trailheads. Off Tom Harvey Road: Turn onto Newbury Drive. Head south and a small lot is on the right. Off Shore Road (Route 1A), east of Winnapaug Road: Turn onto Newbury Drive headed north, and a parking area is on the right.
Parking: Yes, for several cars at each lot
Dogs: Allowed but must be leashed or under voice control of the owner
Last Date Hiked: October 2022
Trailhead GPS: 41.34332, -71.80639

WESTERLY—From Charlie's Overlook, hikers can peer through the trees to see Winnapaug Pond, the Misquamicut barrier beach, the Atlantic Ocean and—on a crystal-clear day—Block Island.

Named for Charles F. Hickox Jr., the late geologist, outdoorsman and educator, the high point is on a long, rocky ridge, called a moraine, at the southern tip of the Dr. John Champlin Glacier Park. The preserve's other geologic features include a unique set of kames, kettle ponds and erratics that explain how the land was shaped by massive ice sheets that swept across Rhode Island tens of thousands of years ago.

The 134-acre park, and five miles of trails, are named for Champlin, a well-known local doctor and businessman who died in 1938. His estate transferred the land in 2004 to the Westerly Land Trust, which manages the property.

I decided to explore the preserve, and learn more about the glacial geography, by setting out on the orange-blazed trail at a trailhead off Tom Harvey Road. I walked south on a wide, flat path through an area called Chestnut Farm, where more than 50 blight-resistant chestnut tree saplings were planted in 2007. The trail wound through a mixed hardwood forest

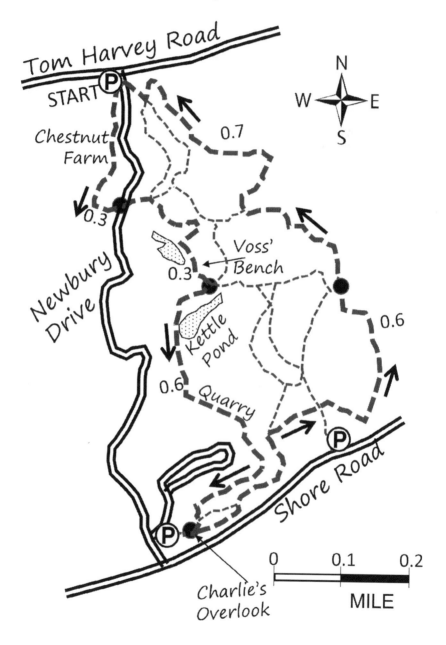

with fields on the right before turning east along the edge of a development called Winnapaug Cottages. The trail then crossed Newbury Drive before reentering the woods.

Coming to a junction, I chose to walk the perimeter of the preserve by picking up the blue-blazed path, one of a network of interconnected, color-coded trails. Just ahead on the right, a side spur opens to what looks like a large field but is a shallow pond that freezes in the winter and is used by ice skaters and hockey players.

The trail then ran along and through gaps in several stone walls. Before the Europeans settled here and built the walls to mark property lines or enclose livestock, the Niantic and Narragansett tribes for thousands of years lived, farmed, fished, and hunted along the coast.

At one point, the trail climbs a small ridge to a rustic bench that faces west. Called Voss' Bench, the site is a tribute to Voss Hutton (1909-2003), requested by his daughter, Cynthia Lafferty, the first president of the Westerly Land Trust. Above the bench, a sign is lettered with an Irish blessing. It begins, "May the road rise up to meet you," and ends with, "And until we meet again, May God hold you in the palm of his hand."

After sitting there for a few minutes, I continued on the path that ran downhill to a pool on the left that was surrounded by a grassy rim. The circular body of water is a kettle pond, formed when a receding glacier stagnated, and a huge chunk of ice broke off and settled in the ground. As it melted, the kettle pond was formed. The pool, below the groundwater table, is not fed by brooks or streams. The glaciers also left small mounds of gravel called kames around the pond.

After studying the pond, I kept going on the blue-blazed path and passed several scatterings of granite stones with sharp edges. These were different from the huge, rounded boulders, called erratics, that were deposited by the retreating and melting glaciers. This set of gray blocks was left from a quarrying operation, probably in the late 1700s or early 1800s.

The quarry workers used a technique called "plug and feather" boulder quarrying to cut bedrock and erratics into the rectangular shapes with square corners that were used for construction. They drilled holes every few inches in a straight line across the rock by using a plug or star drill and a hammer. Two shims, called feathers, were inserted in the hole and a plug was wedged between the feathers to split the stone. Broken or partially defective quarry stones were left behind, and the practice was replaced by the 1870s by more efficient deep pit, commercial quarrying.

After inspecting the stones, I continued following the trail up and down ridges, with houses visible through the trees on the right. The trail reached Charlie's Overlook, named for Hickox, who helped create the preserve and develop the trails.

I sat in the sun on a smooth erratic, took in the view of Block Island Sound and studied several educational signs posted at the overlook. I learned that from 15,000 to 21,000 years ago, a series of glaciers crept down from Canada and covered Rhode Island and points south.

The ice sheets, some several miles thick, acted like bulldozers that scraped and dug through the terrain while pushing soil, sand, gravel, and boulders in front of them.

When one of the glaciers halted and began to melt, it dropped what it was pushing to form a ridgeline, called a terminal moraine. That moraine stretches from Long Island to Nantucket and helped shape Block Island.

After that glacier receded, another swept down from the north but didn't get as far south as the earlier ice sheet and formed another ridge, called a recessional moraine, that runs through Westerly and Charlestown and along the coast northeast to Narragansett. The ridge I walked on in Champlin Glacier Park is part of the recessional moraine.

From Charlie's Outlook, I could see that the glaciers also left an outwash plain, a gently sloping deposit of sand, gravel and sediment that was flushed from the front of the glaciers by runoff streams.

Past the outlook, a short path downhill led to a trailhead, information kiosk, parking lot and a development of senior citizen condominiums at the south end of Newbury Drive.

I returned to Charlie's Outlook and headed northeast on a trail that parallels Shore Road. I learned later that along the road was once farmland, and the Oaks Inn, which included a restaurant, resort, and stables where guests could ride horses. A nearby polo field was used by people from Watch Hill.

After the attack on Pearl Harbor, the U.S. military seized the property and set up a shoreline defense to monitor enemy submarines and protect the coast. Placements for four 155 mm guns were installed on the glacial

A circular kettle pond was formed when a chunk of ice broke off a melting glacier and left a water-filled depression in the ground.

moraine, and the old inn was used as a barracks for the soldiers.

After following the road for a short distance, the trail ducked into the woods and crossed several side spurs. I stayed on the blue-blazed trail, which ran below a high ridge on the right before picking up the green-dot trail. The path ran along the edge of the preserve, flanked a valley on the left and then ran northwest back to the trailhead.

I had a little more time and took the white-blazed trail south and found a dried-up, leaf-covered vernal pool. By late winter and early spring, the depression will fill with runoff from snowmelt and groundwater and become a breeding ground for amphibians and invertebrates, including frogs, toads, salamanders and fairy shrimp. At that point, I turned around and retraced my steps to the trailhead.

During some research after my hike, I read that Hickox, a Westerly native who became a geology professor, would often lead small groups across the preserve and up and down the moraine to explain how the glaciers shaped the land. The terrain is a perfect, outdoor classroom for his lectures.

5 Mount Hope Farm

A hike into Colonial and tribal history along the Bay

Distance: 2.8 miles
Time: 90 minutes
Difficulty: Easy on mostly paved roads

Access: Off Route 136, just north of Roger Williams University, turn east and drive down a short road to the farm.
Parking: Available at large lots
Dogs: Not allowed
Last Date Hiked: August 2022
Trailhead GPS: 41.67008, -71.25700

BRISTOL—The short, shaded, side spur gradually descended through an opening in the trees to a salt marsh on the shore of Church Cove.

The view was spectacular. To the southwest, the Mount Hope Bridge glistened in the early-morning sun. To the south, a powerboat droned across the cove, kicking up sea spray. To the southeast, Seal Island jutted out of the water, covered with white seagulls.

I found the sweeping vista while walking through Mount Hope Farm, the 127-acre property owned by the nonprofit Mount Hope Trust. The parcel of land, located on the eastern shore of Bristol, overlooks the part of Narragansett Bay known as Mount Hope Bay.

For thousands of years, the wooded promontory was inhabited by the Pokanokets until the tribe was driven off the land by English settlers and farmers. The name "Mount Hope," referring to a 209-foot hill and the highest point in Bristol, is derived from the Pokanoket word Montaup, which means "rock shore" or "lookout place."

I set out to explore the farm—and learn some history—after parking in a lot behind a restored 19th-century barn topped with a glass cupola and a weathervane in the shape of a horse. I walked south along a stone wall on a path that circled historic farm buildings and then continued across a large, mowed pasture to reach a paved road. I took it east down a long, gentle slope.

The view from the shoreline of Church Cove includes the Mount Hope Bridge in the distance.

After winding through a mixed forest, the shaded road flattened and passed a huge, golden-colored hay field on the left with milkweed, black-eyed Susans and other wildflowers growing at its edges.

Further along the road, I passed a side trail and then took the next dirt path on the right. It led me south to the banks of Church Cove, with its stunning views of the bridge, boats, the island, and houses across the water in Portsmouth. Under a clear blue sky, a wisp of a salty sea breeze blew from the cove across my face.

I returned to the main trail and headed north. I came to a junction and stayed right, passing several stone-lined channels built to carry runoff from the hillside through seasonal brooks to the Bay. Greenish, weathered plaques bolted to the stones told me the structures were built in 1939 by the federal Works Progress Administration (WPA).

I followed the road to Cove Cabin, an Adirondack-style log structure built in the early 20th century by Rudolph Haffenreffer, an industrialist whose family once owned the Herreshoff Manufacturing Co. and the Narragansett Brewing Co.

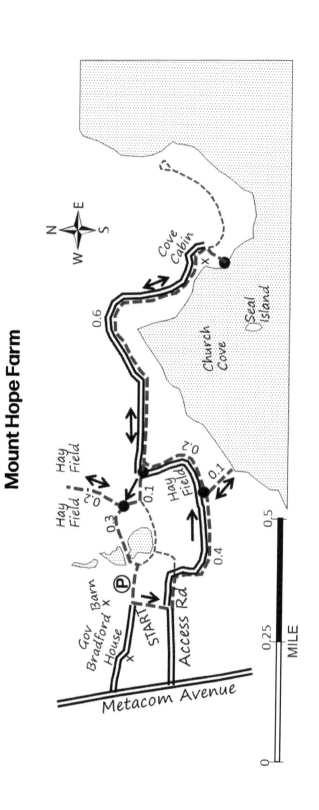

The site is now used for weddings and special events, and I wandered by some huge white tents put up along a rocky shore with a cobble beach. An American flag fluttered in the breeze on a pole behind the cottage. Some wooden pilings just offshore may have once been part of a boat dock.

I rested under shady trees on a wooden bench overlooking the Bay and pulled out my binoculars to study the Mount Hope Bridge, completed at a cost of $5 million in 1929. You can see cars crossing the long, two-lane suspension bridge with 285-foot towers.

In the foreground, I spotted the smooth, rounded rock called Seal Island. Hikers report seeing harbor seals sunning themselves on the rocks in the winter and sometimes ospreys in the spring and blue herons in the summer.

As I looked at the hillside that runs down to the ocean and makes up Mount Hope Farm, I thought some more about its history. The territory was once ruled by Massasoit Ousamequin, the great sachem of the Pokanoket Nation. He considered the land sacred and the tribe's birthright.

After his death, one of his sons, King Philip, also known as Metacomet, led the Pokanokets, the headship tribe of about 60 clans, tribes, and bands in the region. He made Mount Hope his base of operations during King Philip's War (1675-1676), a brutal, bloody conflict that erupted with the English settlers.

Just to the northeast of the farm is King Philips' Chair, a rocky quartz and granite ledge that spills out of the hillside. It was used for ceremonies and as a lookout for enemy ships on Mount Hope Bay. The property is now owned by Brown University. Nearby is Misery Swamp, where Colonists shot and killed King Philip.

After his death, the remaining Pokanokets were enslaved, killed, or driven off the land, and the prized property was claimed at various times by Plymouth Colony, Massachusetts Bay Colony, and Rhode Island. Eventually, the land passed through several owners, including the Church, Bradford and Haffenreffer families.

Today, the Mount Hope Farm property ends just east of the cabin, and after a long rest, a snack, and some water, I decided to retrace my steps on the road. At the junction at the hay field that I had passed before, I went right and climbed a small hillside until I stopped at a bench under a tree

Mount Hope Farm in Bristol features several large hay fields that provide habitat for ground animals and birds.

on the edge of the field. Walkers report seeing rafters of wild turkeys here, and the tall grasses hide mice, moles, foxes, fishers, and minks.

Continuing on the road, I took a side path on the right and walked between two more square-shaped hayfields that are sanctuaries for nesting birds, songbirds, and wildlife. Just to the west, I walked by a series of three small ponds. Two of the ponds were covered with lily pads, cat-o-nine tails, tall reeds, and grasses while the third, lower pond was home to ducks, geese, and a pair of swans.

I passed between two of the shallow ponds and found a cement spillway for water to drain from one to the other. But during this summer's drought, there wasn't a trickle.

Haffenreffer, who bought the farm in 1917, built a duck blind on one of the ponds. He also raised and released pheasants that he and his friends hunted. Hunting is no longer allowed on the property. I learned later that Haffenreffer had expanded the network of ponds with the help of the WPA.

It's unclear why the public agency worked on private land.

Following the road, I passed lines of neat stone walls before returning to the lot where I started. Several groups of youngsters had arrived in the meantime to visit the pens of chickens, dwarf goats and miniature donkeys. Others were playing tag on a hillside.

I decided to explore the complex of buildings, including a greenhouse, guest house, tool shed and groundskeeper's house. I paused at the Governor Bradford House, built by Isaac Royall in 1745. The house is named for William Bradford, the great-great grandson of Puritan Governor William Bradford and a former deputy governor of Rhode Island and U.S. senator. He lived on the farm and invited George Washington to spend a night there in 1790. While circling the house, I noted the walled garden and unusual beech and sequoia trees before returning to where I had parked.

Walkers, joggers, families, and visitors will find easy-to-follow roads and trails up and down hillsides and along the Bay at Mount Hope Farm. There's also plenty of important history to learn along the way.

Water tumbles from Hawkins Pond over a terraced, smooth-stone dam built into an earthen dike.

A lumber and woodworking mill once ran on power generated from the water flowing from Hawkins Pond.

6 Hawkins Pond

The electrifying past of land that once sustained mills

Distance: 3 miles
Time: 90 minutes
Difficulty: Easy, flat loop trails

Access: Head west on Route 44 from Chepachet. Drive about six miles and the trailhead is on the right, just before the state line.
Parking: Available at two small lots
Dogs: Allowed, but must be kept on a leash
Last Date Hiked: June 2021
Trailhead GPS: 41.91740, -71.79360

GLOCESTER—Walter Hawkins was an entrepreneur who learned from his ancestors that waterpower could be harnessed to cut lumber and run woodworking mills.

Hawkins, a self-taught mechanic, installed a generator below a spillway from a man-made pond in 1912 and created electricity to light his house, and later small parts of West Glocester and nearby Connecticut. The system was sold to Narragansett Electric in the 1930s.

Today, Hawkins Pond bears his family's name and is the center of three, short, forested loop trails. The Glocester Land Trust acquired much of the property in 1993 from a member of the Hawkins family and dedicated the blazed trails in 2021.

The 75-acre preserve abuts Pulaski Park, a part of the 4,000-acre George Washington Management Area. Just to the north is Buck Hill State Management Area. Local conservationists hope that together, the area may be large enough to apply for National Wilderness status, a prestigious federal designation for such a small state.

I set out from a small parking lot off Putnam Pike. There's a fireplace and stone terrace near the trailhead on a grassy hillside and to the north you can see a long earthen dam that holds back a quiet 10-acre pond. Just below the dam are the remains of the old mills, including some of the stone walls, brick window casings and concrete floors.

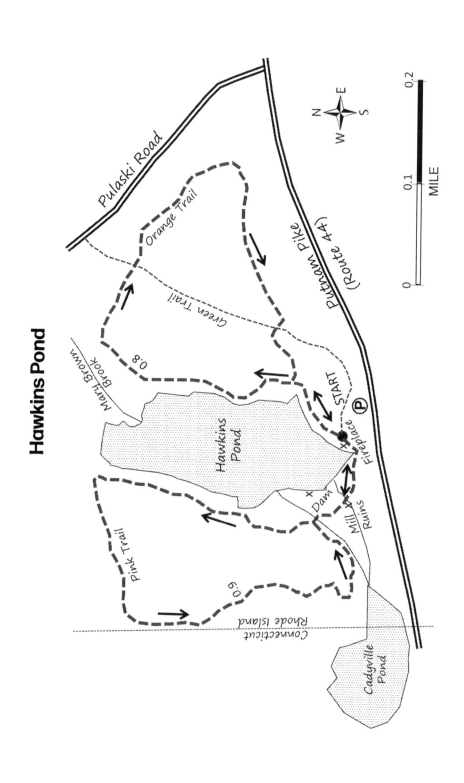

Walter Hawkins' father, Allen, built the dam to create the waterflow to run the family's mill that cut lumber and turned out a variety of wood products.

I walked a hundred yards along the top of the man-made dike to a lovely, 15-foot, terraced, smooth-stone waterfall. Benches along the top of the dike offered views of the lily-pad covered pond that locals considered to be a good fishing spot.

From there, I walked down the impoundment and picked up the fern-covered, pink-blazed trail that hugs the pond before heading west into the woods under tall pines to the border with Connecticut. It circled back across stone walls to a stream that empties from the waterfall and eventually forms another small pond at the state border.

Back at the trailhead, I walked north on the orange trail that crossed a brook and edged the east side of the water before reaching Mary Brown Brook, which feeds the pond and was named for a woman who lived in the woods there in the 1880s.

Upstream, beavers have built a dam, creating a large pool. There's a bench to look for the beavers and other wildlife and waterfowl. Hikers report the preserve attracts pheasant, turkeys, deer, fox, coyotes, porcupines, raccoons, muskrats, woodchucks and opossum. Fishermen say the otters have reduced the number of fish in the pond.

At this point, the trail turns east up a ridge and crosses the green-blazed trail on the right before looping back toward the trailhead. I passed a toppled telephone pole with transformers that once carried electricity to Clarkville and houses along Pulaski Road. There's also an old wooden shed where the laborers at the mill took shelter.

The trail then crosses a series of small dikes built on streams before rising gently along a ridgeline and returning to where I started.

In all, I hiked about 3 miles for about 90 minutes, including a mile on the pink trail, 0.8 miles on the orange trail, a short hop on the green trail and other wanderings along and around the dike.

As I was leaving, a mother and a young girl arrived for a walk along the top of the earthen dam. The mom told me her daughter liked to explore. I replied that she found the right place.

Extensive stonework, including a stone-lined earthen dike, holds back water that flows over a dam in the Moshassuck River Preserve.

7 Moshassuck River Preserve

Skipping across streams and a rich mill history

Distance: 3 miles
Time: 2 hours
Difficulty: Easy to moderate, with several steep climbs and stream crossings

Access: Off Route 123 in Lincoln, take Great Road north. Turn left on Sherman Avenue to the trailhead.
Parking: Available for 15 cars
Dogs: Allowed, but must be leashed
Last Date Hiked: January 2022
Trailhead GPS: 41.91453, -71.44272

LINCOLN—Every new year should start with a hike on a fresh trail that has interesting natural and man-made features that make you pause and think.

I found one in the Moshassuck River Preserve on the banks of a historic waterway with stonework from another era, giant glacial boulders, and a hardwood forest. The name, Moshassuck, is a Native American term for "river where the moose waters."

The undeveloped land has been hiked by locals for decades. But in September 2021, The Nature Conservancy opened two public loop trails to relieve overcrowding in other areas near Greater Providence as more Rhode Islanders wanted to get outdoors to walk during the pandemic.

The 210-acre preserve is a good example of a collaboration among the nonprofit Nature Conservancy and abutting private landowners to give people an easy walk in the woods.

The trailhead of the preserve opens between the first tee of the Fairlawn Country Club and a small grove of oak, hickory, and maple trees. The golf club built the parking lot for free and provided a small excavator and crew to install signs at an information kiosk.

The path starts down a short slope and crosses a stone bridge over the Moshassuck River, which flows for 8.9 miles south from Lime Rock Preserve

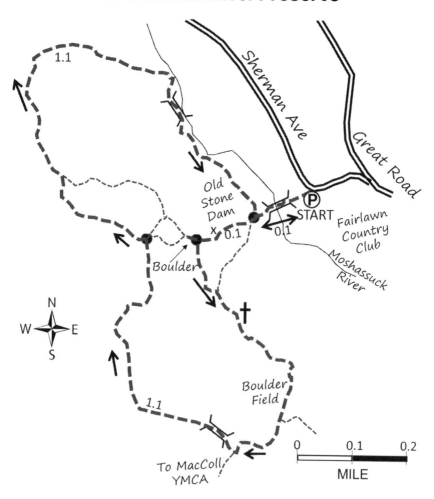

in Lincoln to Providence, where it converges with the Woonasquatucket River to form the Providence River.

Just north of the bridge is some extensive stonework with a 100-foot-long, 8-foot-high stone-lined earthen dike. The impoundment holds back a pond, and, at one end, water flows over a dam, creating a waterfall before flowing south and under the bridge.

I'm not sure who built the dam or what its original purpose was. It may have been an old mill site, one of many built for waterpower along the Moshassuck, such as the Butterfly Factory. The long-closed cotton mill that opened a half mile downstream in 1811 is named for the way the stones in the walls were pieced together in a butterfly shape.

The stonework in the preserve may have been built in the mid-1800s to control the water flow for large mills downriver, such as the Sayles Bleachery, a textile finishing mill in Saylesville. The impoundment could have held back water to protect flooding at the mills or to create a reservoir to be released during dry seasons.

After exploring the site, I walked up a small hill to a fork in the trail and a huge boulder balanced on a smaller stone. It doesn't seem like a natural formation and may have been built by Native Americans as a marker or by someone later to mimic that type of structure.

At the split, I went left on the yellow-blazed trail through what was once a Boy Scout property called Camp Conklin, which was supported by the Conklin Limestone Company and where Troop 64 held outdoor activities. The Nature Conservancy acquired 125 acres, or more than half the preserve, from the company.

Just ahead and off the trail is a small amphitheater with benches, a firepit and a memorial built in 1984 for Prudy Hayden, a leader of Cub Scout Pack 1 in Saylesville.

The trail continues along a ridgeline, up and down several hillsides and across tributaries of the Moshassuck. At the bottom of a gentle slope is a small historic cemetery with several small headstones almost buried under the leaves. I couldn't read any of the engravings on the stones.

The trail passes through a field of glacial erratics before turning west along the edge of the preserve. I could see on higher ground to the left the back of some buildings on Breakneck Hill Road. At the edge of the

A wooden slat bridge crosses a feeder stream that runs east to the Moshassuck River.

preserve, the MacColl YMCA allowed hikers to follow existing paths on its private property rather than require The Nature Conservancy to cut new trails on the preserve.

Several signs on trees identify the property boundaries.

A dirt road that may have been an old farm lane or cart path enters the preserve from a hillside on the left, and hikers follow it over a wide bridge. A round culvert channels water below it. Don't miss the split glacial boulder and the lean-to shelter built of tree trunks and branches between the rocks on the left.

The trail soon bends north over a wooden bridge and along a stone wall within the sights and sounds of Route 146 just to the west.

At an intersection, a white-blazed trail on the right leads back to the trailhead. I stayed straight on the blue-blazed trail, which crossed more streams, edged a vernal pool, and ran through a wet, mucky area and what looked like an old well or section of culvert. The path turned east and down a long, steep slope back to the Moshassuck River.

I stopped, rested, and thought about the river's rich history. Roger Williams founded the original settlement of Providence in 1636 on the east bank of the Moshassuck. That area is now Roger Williams Memorial Park near the city's downtown.

During the 1700s, the banks of the river were filled with tanneries, grist mills, slaughterhouses, distilleries, a paper mill, and a chocolate factory.

In the 1800s, dozens of textile and manufacturing mills built on the river fueled the Industrial Revolution.

Now, there are 11 dams, a reservoir and five ponds along the river's course.

From the riverbank, I could see a well-constructed bridge on private property just to the north and the remains of foundations with iron rods and stone slabs that once supported other bridges over the waterway.

An old cabin and a wooden bridge that once stood near the stone slabs were removed by The Nature Conservancy for safety reasons.

I followed the trail along the riverbank and crossed some plank bridges to reach the stonework I had visited earlier. I spent a few more minutes studying the construction before returning to the trailhead.

By my count during my hike, the preserve is crisscrossed by 10 feeder streams, tributaries and rivulets that run toward the Moshassuck River. I rock-hopped and jumped over a few. I crossed another one on a split tree trunk someone had laid over the water. The Nature Conservancy plans to erect more small bog and foot bridges to help first-time hikers navigate the preserve.

That will be a good addition, if the river, and the land on its banks with its long history stays as it is.

A bench on a high earthen dam overlooks upper Chace Pond where visitors can see ducks, geese, muskrats, and other wildlife.

Benjamin Simmons built an extensive dam and stone-lined raceway in the 18th century to power his sawmill and gristmill.

8 Simmons Mill Pond Management Area

A pristine preserve perfect for a leisurely stroll

Distance: 3.5 miles
Time: 2.5 hours
Difficulty: Easy, on flat paved roads and dirt paths

Access: Take Route 179 to Adamsville and turn west on Cold Brook Road (also known as Colebrook Road). Drive to 212 Cold Brook Road and the trailhead is on the left.
Parking: Available in a lot
Dogs: Allowed, but must be leashed
Last Date Hiked: April 2021
Trailhead GPS: 41.53994, -71.15411

LITTLE COMPTON—Benjamin Simmons dammed Cold Brook in the mid-1700s to create a pond and raceways to harness the waterpower to run his gristmill. The mill is long gone, but the pond became the center of a natural sanctuary for birds and wildlife.

In the 1960s, Bill Chace and his family built five more ponds connected with a network of trails. The Chace family sold the land in 1995 to the Rhode Island Department of Environmental Management, which maintains the family-friendly public preserve.

Today, the 433-acre refuge, named the Simmons Mill Pond Management Area, is unique because of the wide, easy-to-walk trails and dozens of hand-lettered signs identifying trees, wildlife, rock formations and the land's rich history.

It's a favorite of folks in the East Bay. After hearing about it for years, I decided to visit and set out from a small lot on Cold Brook Road, off Route 179 in the village of Adamsville, on a clear, early-spring morning with temperatures in the 50s.

I stopped at the kiosk at the trailhead to study a rough map and noticed along the trail dozens of informative signs, many on stumps for easy reading

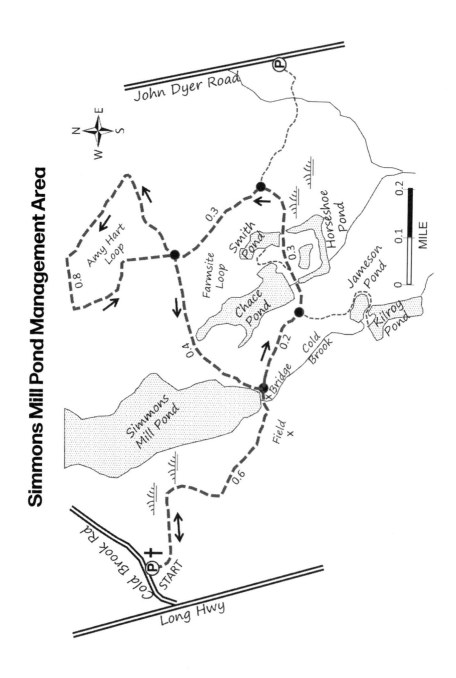

by youngsters. One read: "The trunk of this large red oak was weakened by fungi and carpenter ants. Gale force winds shattered it."

There are also customized pooper scoopers on wooden sticks to keep the trails clean. Volunteers Gail and Roger Greene provided many of the enhancements.

At the start, the gravel road slopes gently downhill. In the wetlands on the left, I heard the loud, quacking-like sounds of wood frogs that have emerged from the long winter. I also saw dozens of bird nesting boxes, made from logs naturally hollowed out by decay and insects. There are wooden benches on which to rest, listen and watch the forest.

After a half mile, the trail opens to a flat, grassy area on the banks of the 18-acre Simmons Pond that is stocked with trout in the spring. Water flows from the pond under the dam Simmons built into Cold Brook. Below the dike, the remains are visible of the stone-lined raceways designed to power Simmons' sawmill and gristmill for grinding grains, cow corn and flint corn for jonnycakes.

The trail then splits into the Farmsite Loop. I took the right fork through a rare coastal Atlantic oak-holly woodland—a narrow band of holly and oak trees that hugs the coast from Long Island to Massachusetts and grows in moderate temperatures along the shore.

In a hundred yards or so, an overgrown side trail on the right once led to two ponds—Jameson and Kilroy—and a small dam, where the overflow spills into Cold Brook. But the path is no longer maintained and I stayed on the Farmsite Loop.

Around the next turn, I found two ponds. Water from the upper Chace Pond tumbled down a cement spillway to the lower Horseshoe Pond. I sat on a bench on a high earthen dam above Chace Pond and spied two ducks among the wood duck boxes on the far end. Hikers report seeing geese, ospreys, and herons, as well as deer, minks, foxes, muskrats, and raccoons.

Back on the main trail, a side path on the left leads to Smith Pond, where anglers catch bass, pickerel, crappie, and sunfish. There's marshland on the right.

I passed another side spur to a second parking area off John Dyer Road.

Up a slight grade, I found stone walls, animal pens and a capped, stone-lined well—remains from the Hambly Farm.

At the next intersection, the Amy Hart loop opens on the right and circles through heavy forest and back to the junction. Ox carts once used the lanes to haul firewood from the woodlots. I took a right, crossed a spot with water running over the trail, and reached the shores of Simmons Pond.

I inspected the foundation of an old icehouse landing and rested on a bench within sight of the Simmons dam. The Chace family in the 1950s built a cabin here that was later taken down. I watched trout swimming in the pond and remembered the trees in the preserve—red maple, beech, sassafras, black gum, and yellow birch.

It was time to head back, and just after the dam I took a side loop on the left through a field before returning to the gravel road to the trailhead.

The Simmons Mill Pond sanctuary is quiet and pristine, with open, flat lanes for leisurely strolls and much to see and learn.

9   The Monastery

On secluded and serene paths where Trappist monks once walked

Distance: 4.5 miles
Time: 2.5 hours
Difficulty: Mostly easy flat paths with some moderate hills and ridges

Access: At the intersection with Route 295, take Route 114 south and drive 3 miles to the driveway to the monastery on the right.
Parking: Available at several lots
Dogs: Allowed, but must be leashed
Last Date Hiked: July 2022
Trailhead GPS: 41.93364, -71.40360

CUMBERLAND—Trappist monks once toiled in silence in the quarries, orchards, vegetable gardens, pastures and hay fields on the land that surrounded their monastery.

At the end of the workday, they followed the roads, cart paths and farm lanes back to their abbey. Some would have passed the monument they had rebuilt to memorialize Nine Men's Misery, the name of the burial site where centuries before Colonists were killed by Native Americans during a brutal war.

The monks erected the monastery after they arrived in 1902 and lived, worked, and prayed on the grounds until 1950, when a fire destroyed several of their buildings and they left for a new home in Spencer, Massachusetts.

Later, the Town of Cumberland acquired and preserved the remaining structures and the adjacent 481 acres of hilly, wooded, and swampy land, including the paths where the monks had once walked.

The sanctuary now includes a maze of 7.5 miles of trails, many of them unmarked. Some of the color-coded blazes that once identified paths have faded. So, hikers can wander and find their own way on a quiet, contemplative walk, similar to the ones taken by the monks many years ago.

I parked near the Cumberland Public Library, one of the monks' old buildings that the town renovated and then set out south on a hard-packed

The Monastery

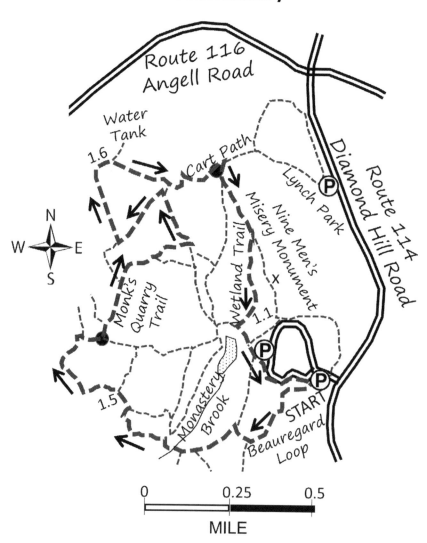

dirt path called the Beauregard Loop. The wide, 1.2-mile trail circles the library and other public buildings through the woods and is shared by walkers, joggers, trail runners and families with children. I saw two moms pushing babies in strollers.

I passed a field on the right and decided to leave the Beauregard Trail to walk the perimeter of the property. At a junction, I went left through a heavily wooded area, passed some wetlands and crossed Monastery Brook, which bisects the land and flows south to the Blackstone River.

A narrow footpath covered in ferns opened on the left, and I took it to the edge of a large swamp, covered in places with green algae and teeming with wildlife.

I paused to watch a beaver swim toward a den it had built among some dead trees and small islands in the shallow water. A raft of mallard and wood ducks cruised across the surface, often bobbing for food. Hundreds of birds, some tweeting and calling, filled the branches of the trees.

It is quite an unusual, secluded place, and I wondered if the monks had visited the marshy habitat to contemplate nature and its relationship to their spiritual life.

I followed the banks of the swamp, and at one point the path dipped down into a gully, filled with branches. Somebody had stretched a rope between trees on both sides of the gap for hikers to hold onto to navigate the uneven path.

The trail eventually turned inland from the marsh, crossed through some gaps in stone walls and led to a wider path called "Monk's Quarry Trail."

I climbed uphill and then walked along a long, flat, raised causeway of earth and stones. Near the end of the berm, I spotted an area littered with rectangular stone slabs and posts, some covered with thick green moss, leaves, or lichens. This was the quarry where the monks cut the "pigeon gray" granite blocks that they had used to build the monastery. I found some old tracks that may have been laid to transport carts loaded with the heavy stones.

Back on the trail I turned north at the next intersection on a path that looped northwest around what was once an apple orchard. The monks tended cherry trees on the land.

Trappist monks cut granite blocks from a quarry on the property to build their monastery in Cumberland. The sculpture in the foreground shows a hand clasping a prayer book.

At this point, the trail runs to a fence line, and I found a side spur to a series of cliffs that overlook a large, private working sandpit and quarry. Far to the southwest, I could see the tops of the tall buildings in downtown Providence.

When I went back to the trail, I was met by chipmunks, squirrels and field mice scurrying across the path. I started to head east along the Cart Path Trail, which eventually leads to Lynch Park on Diamond Hill Road.

Well before reaching that point, I saw a red blaze and turned right onto the Nine Men's Misery Trail. After a short distance, huge, grassy meadows opened on the right, covered with wildflowers and milkweed, and buzzing with bees.

Farther down the trail, on a small, wooded knoll on the left, is a solid, rectangular stack of rocks and cement. In front of it is a granite pillar with a plaque that marks the burial site of nine soldiers slain in March 1676 after "Pierce's Fight."

Capt. Michael Pierce led the local militia during King Philip's War

The Nine Men's Misery monument marks a burial ground for soldiers killed during King Philip's War.

(1675-1676), the conflict between the Colonists and Native Americans, marked by savagery on both sides. Pierce and many of his men were ambushed and killed at a bend in the Blackstone River. Nine soldiers escaped and made their way north, only to be captured, tortured and slain.

Their burial site was originally marked in 1676 with a simple cairn of stones. In 1928, the monks built the rectangular structure, and the state later put up the pillar and plaque. It's believed to be the oldest veterans' memorial in the country.

I paused there respectfully for a few minutes before returning to the main trail. I turned west and then south on the blue-blazed Wetland Trail, which passed a field on the left and a marsh on the right before reaching a pond that the monks used to irrigate vegetable gardens. In the winter, they cut ice blocks there.

The trail eventually heads south, crosses the Beauregard Loop and returns to the back of the monastery through fields where the monks once grazed cattle and another large area called Green Acres Meadow.

From there, it was just a short walk on a paved road that circled the monastery to where I had parked. The last leg of the hike gave me a chance to study the buildings and grounds where as many as 135 monks at a time lived, worked and prayed.

I noted the thick, granite walls, a wide staircase on one side that led to a locked iron gate, a sculpture on the lawn of a hand clasping a prayer book and a tall tower with a housing for a bell that rang to summon the monks back from the fields.

As I finished my walk, I thought more about the monks' vows of poverty, chastity, obedience and silence during a lifetime of manual labor, prayer, spiritual readings and reflection. Their discipline and dedication to a monastic life is impressive.

There's plenty to think about as you wander through the remote woods and isolated marshes with only your thoughts and the monks' history to guide you. After all these years, the monastery remains a refuge for quiet contemplation, and in chaotic times, that's just what all of us need.

10   Haile Farm Preserve

On the lookout for ospreys and eagles along the Palmer River

Distance: 2 miles
Time: 90 minutes
Difficulty: Easy with some wet areas

Access: Off Market Street (Route 136), turn west at the sign for Haile Farm and drive through a small industrial area to the trailhead.
Parking: Available for a few cars
Dogs: Allowed, but must be leashed
Last Date Hiked: October 2022
Trailhead GPS: 41.751110, -71.27453

WARREN—Rock Singewald gestures across the wide, flat marshland where farmers for hundreds of years swung scythes to harvest salt hay to use as livestock fodder and to sell in local markets.

The salt hay became a valuable crop for generations of families that farmed along the Palmer River, says Singewald, president of the Warren Land Conservation Trust, which manages the Haile Farm Preserve.

The nonprofit group maintains a network of trails through the 61-acre sanctuary that includes wooded uplands and paths to the river, where hikers can cross the marsh and see salt sparrows, ospreys and, if you're lucky, an eagle soaring overhead.

On a crystal-clear early morning, Singewald and I walked the trails at Haile Farm after driving through a small industrial area off Market Street to the trailhead near the entrance of Jade, a local manufacturer. We began by heading west on a right-of-way through private property that is covered in places with wood chips.

The trail entered a dense area of invasive plants, including autumn olive, bittersweet, multiflora rose and mugwort that crowd out native species unless they are cut back. The terrain changed from bushes to stands of boxelder and a few gray birch trees. We crossed a red maple swamp on board bridges built by volunteers and local Boy Scouts.

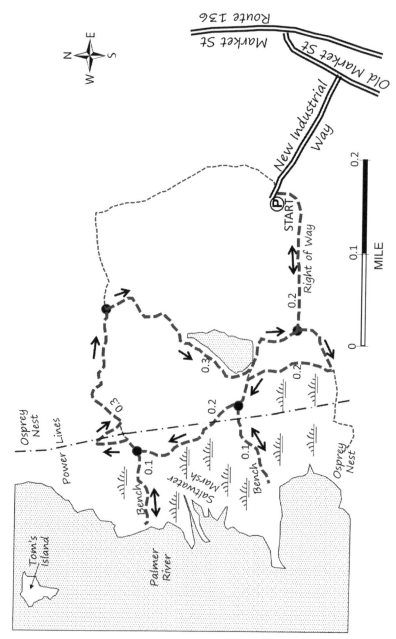

Turning left on the red-blazed trail, we paused at a small, interesting circle of tall, quaking aspen trees and then continued through some fallen trees blown down by heavy winds.

A blue-blazed trail on the left would have taken us to the river but was closed to protect ospreys and their nests.

The area turned wet, and we crossed bog bridges through patches of cinnamon ferns and witch hazel before turning from the red-blazed trail, named for Betty Hallberg, onto the green-blazed trail, named for Dick Hallberg. The Hallbergs founded the Warren Land Conservation Trust.

A short distance later, we took a left on a trail that ran over some raised land covered with pitch pines and other small trees and shrubs. We passed a bench and then walked down to the salt marsh on the eastern shore of the Palmer River, a brackish waterway that flows south into the Barrington River and then the Warren River before reaching the ocean.

Along the shore to the left is a wooden pole topped with an osprey nest.

To the south is downtown Warren and the old brick American Tourister Factory. To the east across the placid river are tree-lined banks and some cottages in Barrington.

As far as the eye can see from the marsh, and beyond, the Pokanoket, led by Massasoit Ousamequin, lived for thousands of years on the rich land called Sowams. The Native Americans planted the area upland from the marsh with corn, beans, and squash, fertilized with fish from the river.

After the brutal King Philip's War (1675-1676) between the settlers and Native Americans, the remainder of the tribe was driven off the land, which was divided and parceled out to English Colonists, according to a history by Barbara Andrews Hail, of Warren, a descendant of the Haile family.

In 1682, Obadiah Bowen, the first landowner, built a story-and-a-half farmhouse with a steeply pitched gable roof that still stands off Market Street (Route 136) near the entrance of the preserve. Bowen sold the land in 1708 to Richard Haile, whose family farmed it for about 170 years.

In the mid-1800s, the property was called Judge Haile Farm after Levi Haile, an 1821 Brown University graduate who served as a justice on the Rhode Island Supreme Court. That's the court that tried Thomas Dorr, the leader of the Dorr Rebellion in 1842.

Later, Manual Nunes ran the farm from 1911 to 1988. After a developer abandoned plans to build condos there, the Town of Warren took the title and turned the property over to the Warren Land Conservation Trust.

Haile Farm was one of many saltwater livestock farms that grew along Narragansett Bay and other shores across New England. The early coastal farmers learned that it was more profitable to raise animals than crops.

A livestock farm required less labor, and the salt hay that grew in the salt marshes and low-lying meadows could be cut to feed cattle and dairy cows or be sold to buyers up and down the coast. Salt hay, supplemented with English hay that was grown in upland meadows, became one of the most valuable crops in the first century of English settlement in New England.

The harvesting of the salt hay usually took place every August. Some of the cut hay was loaded on small, flat-bottomed sailing barges, called gundalows, and shipped downriver to markets. Sometimes, wagons hauled the salt hay over roads built up over the wetlands. The horses that pulled the wagons were fitted with special wide, flat-bottomed shoes so they wouldn't get mired in the marsh. And sometimes the farmers stacked the hay on stands in the marsh called "staddles," which were built by driving stakes into the ground about 2 or 3 feet above the marsh. The salt hay dried there and was carried away on sleds over the frozen marsh in mid-winter to be stored in upland barns.

After discussing that history, Singewald and I retraced our steps back to the green-blazed trail and headed north on a path lined in a few places with yellow thistle, which flowers in the spring.

Tucked in the dense brush on the left is a solar-powered station on a short, wooden pole set up by Rhode Island School of Design students to monitor climate change issues.

Turning left on an orange-blazed trail, we passed another bench before arriving at the river again. Just offshore to the northeast, we could see tiny Tom's Island, also called Three Trees Island. Through the trees to the north, the Swansea Golf Club is visible.

Returning to the green-blazed trail, we took a short, yellow-blazed loop, called Eagle View, across some sandy soil and under power lines that run north and south across the preserve. We spotted more osprey nests, including one on top of a utility pole.

Singewald said eagles can sometimes be seen here perched in the tops

Colonial farmers harvested salt hay from the marshes along the Palmer River to use as livestock fodder. Buildings in downtown Warren can be seen on the horizon on the far side of the river.

A small circle of quaking aspen trees is visible just off one of the trails in the uplands section of Haile Farm Preserve in Warren.

of the trees, but they tend to live on the far western side of the river. After the ospreys leave, though, the eagles spend more time on the eastern side of the river and can be seen sometimes on top of the poles where the osprey build their nests.

Back on the green-blazed trail, we headed east under mature oaks and tupelo trees and along stone walls that once enclosed pastures for the livestock. We passed a line of beech and willow trees. The trail bent south and then ran along the top of an earthen berm on the western edge of a pond. The water was stagnant and covered in places with algae.

Years ago, a housing developer built the dike to form a pond to catch runoff from houses, planned condos and some business to the north and east.

The developer, however, never completed the project, and the polluted water from the pond is draining under the berm to the salt marsh. Singewald said the Warren Land Conservation Trust is planning a remedial action, and looking for funding, to solve the problem.

After studying the pond and the runoff issue, we picked up the red-blazed trail and returned to where we'd started.

Haile Farm Preserve is the largest property managed by the land trust and attracts students, botanists, birders, historians, walkers, and others.

Singewald, a former steward of the preserve, said more work always needs to be done at Haile Farm, including cutting back the invasive species, building more board bridges and solving the pond runoff issue. He hopes the improvements attract more people to enjoy the views and learn about the history.

Nature Walks

Pine-needle covered peninsulas with trail benches offer shady spots to rest and view Tillinghast Pond in West Greenwich.

A wooden observation deck offers a view of the 41-acre Tillinghast Pond, which is surrounded by a large coastal forest that extends from Boston to Washington, D.C.

11   Tillinghast Pond Management Area

Where the woods are never far from a water view

Distance: 4 miles
Time: 2.5 hours
Difficulty: Mostly easy with some moderate hills and ridges

Access: Off Route 102 north, turn onto Plain Meetinghouse Road and drive for 3.5 miles. Turn right onto Plain Road and drive a half mile to the trailhead on the right.
Parking: Available for 24 cars
Dogs: Allowed, but must be leashed
Last Date Hiked: June 2022
Trailhead GPS: 41.64667, -71.75726

WEST GREENWICH—Tillinghast Pond, tranquil and clear on a still summer morning, is at the heart of a network of trails that wind through dense stands of white pine, oak, ash, and maple trees that help form the largest coastal forest from Boston to Washington, D.C.

The paths also pass an abandoned homestead, a historic cemetery and other remnants of farmers and woodcutters who once lived on and worked the land here. They're gone now, though, and beavers, otters, turtles, birds, insects, and other wildlife now dominate the nature preserve.

No matter which trails you take in the sanctuary, the pond never seems far away. Whether you're hiking on a secluded path on a hillside or navigating a long ridge, it's reassuring to peer through the trees and catch a glimpse of the sparkling, calm water.

I drove to Tillinghast Pond off Plain Road and parked at a trailhead on the southern end of the water. A short series of wooden steps that was built as a boat launch leads to the shore, where I took my first good, long look at the 41-acre pond and the surrounding 2,200 acres that make up the Tillinghast Pond Management Area.

The preserve, owned by The Nature Conservancy and co-managed with the Rhode Island Department of Environmental Management and

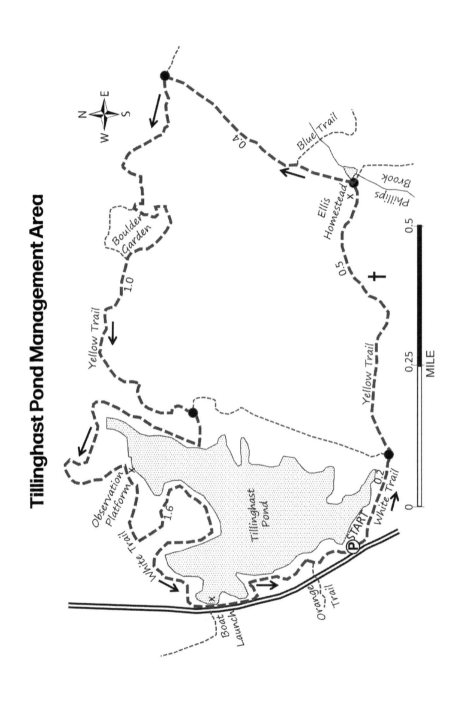

the Town of West Greenwich, is part of a 45,000-acre forest that stretches along the Rhode Island and Connecticut border and makes up the huge area of undeveloped woodlands.

The Nature Conservancy calls it the Wood River Barrens Matrix Forest or the Borderlands Forest, and it includes the Arcadia Management Area, the Pachaug State Forest, and other preserved lands. Permanently conserved in 2006, the Tillinghast Pond Management Area also protects the headwaters of the Wood River, which is part of an extensive watershed and flows south to the Pawcatuck River.

After applying bug spray and pulling on a backpack, I set out from the eastern corner of the parking lot on the white-blazed trail, which runs counterclockwise around the pond. The wide, flat path winds through a thick, white pine forest, runs along some stone walls, and crosses others before reaching a junction.

The white-blazed trail goes left, but I went right on the yellow-blazed Flintlock Trail that crosses land once owned by the Shepard, Bates and Cioe families. The path wanders up and down over several small ridges until following a long gradual downslope past an overgrown cemetery on the right.

The graveyard, circled by a broken stone wall, holds the remains of Wait Ellis (1777-1846) and other family members who, interestingly, all died in the 1820s.

After I respectfully studied the headstones for a few minutes, I returned to the trail and walked a few hundred yards to find what's left of the 1830s-era Ellis Homestead, including a foundation built into a hillside and mostly hidden by wildflowers, tall grass, and a few small trees.

On the right is a small farm pond, lined with long, rectangular stones laid horizontally at the shoreline to retain water. The pond drains under a sturdy stone-slab bridge to form Phillips Brook.

The yellow-blazed trail then turns left and north along a wide, pine-needle covered corridor. I passed two separate blue-blazed trails that opened on the right and led east to the Wickaboxet Management Area.

At another junction, I took a sharp left to go west and the trail rose up a hillside until it split. I went left again and passed through a glacial boulder field before the path ran through a field of sassafras and fragrant wildflowers.

I noted dead oak trees on the hillside that had been defoliated by drought and a spongy moth infestation.

The footpath narrows through a dense stretch of ferns and tall grasses, and I was glad I'd tucked my pants into my socks and put on plenty of bug spray to deter any ticks. The trail led down a slope, and I caught a glimpse of Tillinghast Pond. I walked to the water's edge and scanned the wild, natural shoreline, noting several spots on the banks to pause for views of the water.

Duck boxes and a wooden platform stood on the opposite shore.

I circled the northeast corner of the pond and crossed bog bridges over lowlands and under ash trees. About 30 feet offshore, I noticed a beaver dam that had created a deep cove for the critters.

A little farther on, the path rose over a ridge on the northern side of the pond and passed several outcroppings before reaching a large hay field—one of three, totaling 60 acres, that are mowed regularly by a local farmer under a lease with The Nature Conservancy.

The path skirts the field, with the water on the left, until it reaches a short side spur to the wooden observation platform I'd seen from the other side. Its construction was supported by the Shepard family, which once ran the Shepard Company department store in downtown Providence.

I walked out on the deck and watched butterflies, water bugs, dragonflies, and damselflies just above the surface. Turtles and frogs sunned on partially submerged logs. The water was clear, shallow, and muddy at the bottom. Some of the coves and inlets are covered with lily pads and white water lilies.

The pond is named for the Tillinghasts, a prominent family in West Greenwich who farmed and did some lumbering along Plain Road in the 1800s.

I returned to the yellow-blazed trail, passed another field, and took another side spur to the pond with a sign marked for Howard's Rest, named for Howard White Murre, a humanitarian, naturalist and donor to conservation causes.

Back on the trail, I skirted more fields, spotted houses on a hillside to the right, crossed a stream and passed several small peninsulas that provided trail benches and shady spots to linger while surveying the pond.

At one overlook, I could see Plain Road to the south and a long, low stone and earth dam that ran into the hillside and was apparently built to flood the low area and create the pond.

The trail reached Plain Road, passed a turnout for a few cars and a boat launch, and crossed a small stone bridge above a stream flowing out of the pond and under the road. The water forms Coney Brook as it flows to the Wood River. Beavers sometimes build dams here that must be cleared to keep the road from flooding.

The trail followed the asphalt surface for a couple hundred yards before ducking back into the woods. There's another outlook to the pond on the left and then the path rises on a ridge to the junction with the orange-blazed Coney Brook Trail, which passes under pine, hemlock, and red oak trees and along a brook that runs over a dam and through a ravine. A short, green-blazed side trail, called the Logger's Trail, opens off the Coney Brook Trail and runs through an area that was harvested for timber in 2010 and now teems with birds.

On prior hikes, I've walked those loop trails, but not today. Instead, I decided to head back and followed the yellow-blazed trail a short distance to the parking lot.

At the trailhead, I stopped at the public restroom and read a sign explaining that the composting system uses natural biological decomposition to save 35,000 gallons of water a year and discharges no solid waste or wastewater into the environment.

That's just one small piece of the huge effort over many decades to preserve the sensitive ecology and natural beauty of Tillinghast Pond. It's a lovely place well worth saving.

12   Great Swamp

Discover the majesty of ospreys

Distance: 3.5 miles
Time: 2.5 hours
Difficulty: Easy, mostly flat roads

Access: Off Route 138 in West Kingston, head west on Liberty Lane at a sign for Great Swamp. Follow the road for a couple of miles past the DEM maintenance buildings and a shooting range to a barred gateway.
Parking: Available in a large lot
Dogs: Allowed, but must be leashed
Last Date Hiked: April 2022
Trailhead GPS: 41.47423, -71.57511

SOUTH KINGSTOWN—Two ospreys took flight from their nest on top of a power line tower and soared high into the clouds above Great Swamp.

With wings spread wide, they caught the wind and rose almost out of sight before swooping down across the water, hunting.

On earlier hikes, I've seen the ospreys spot prey, dive feet first into the water and emerge with a fish hooked in their talons before flying back to their nest. But on this walk at midday, the ospreys just soared and gilded majestically high above the swamp.

I found the ospreys at the far end of a loop trail in the Great Swamp Management Area, which is managed by the Rhode Island Department of Environmental Management. Along the way, the trail also passes the remains of a World War II-era seaplane hangar, signs of beaver activity and dense stands of oak and maple trees mixed with tall holly trees.

From a trailhead off Great Neck Road, several friends and I set out to see the ospreys on my first group hike since the Covid-19 pandemic began in March 2020. It felt good to share stories and listen to what caught the interest of my fellow hikers as we walked along.

We started out on a raised gravel road through a swampy area lined with greenbrier vines, bushes, and small trees. At one point, a 12-inch

Great Swamp is home to several ospreys—fish hawks that dive into water to catch prey in their talons.

garter snake slithered across our path and into the brush. Farther on, we spotted gnawed tree stumps where beavers had been at work. The beavers had also tried to clog drains under the road with sticks and mud to back up large pools of water where they live.

Off in the distance, we heard the rumble of Amtrak trains on tracks that run west of the preserve, a counterpoint to the natural world around us.

The road soon reached a fork at a stone marker with a small name plate honoring Dr. John Mulleedy, a late hiking club leader. We went left and passed several shiny, green-leafed holly trees, which stood out from other trees that have yet to open their leaves. After passing under a string of power transmission lines, we noted a large field overgrown with bushes on the right.

It had been cleared of trees and allowed to fill in with shrubs to create a natural habitat for cottontail rabbits, which at one time faced extinction.

We walked to another fork with a stone pillar and plate marked for

Great Swamp

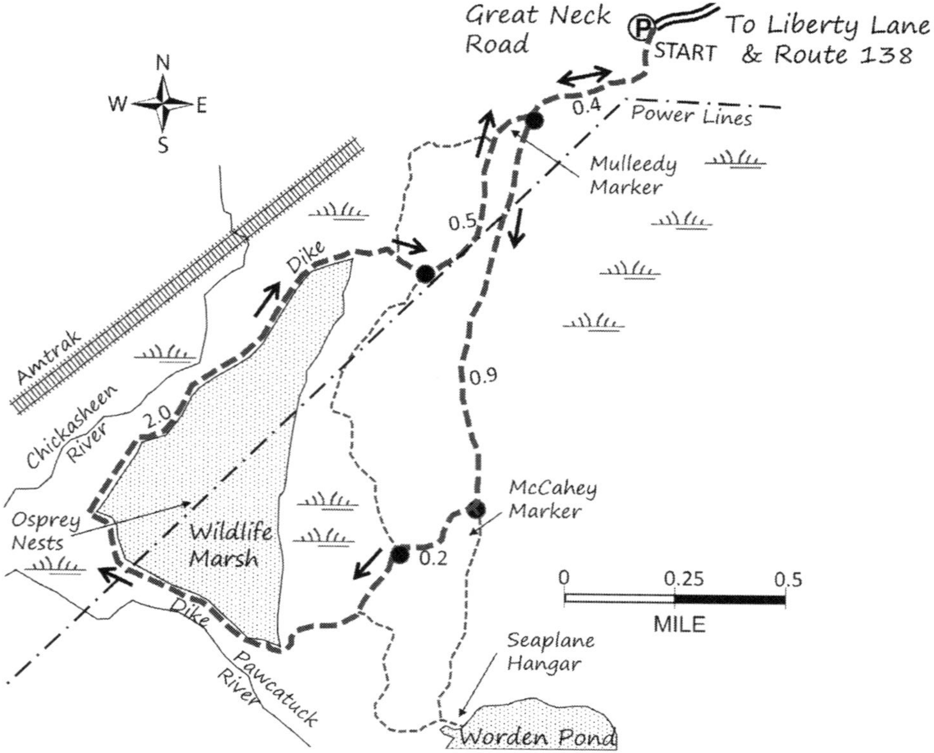

Great Neck Road
To Liberty Lane & Route 138
START
Power Lines
Mulleedy Marker
0.4
0.5
0.9
McCahey Marker
0.2
Seaplane Hangar
Worden Pond
Dike
Wildlife Marsh
Osprey Nests
2.0
Dike
Pawcatuck River
Chickasheen River
Amtrak

N W E S

0 0.25 0.5
MILE

George McCahey, another prominent hiker. The left fork heads down to the northern lip of Worden Pond, a 1,000-acre natural glacial lake. In the past, I've tried to take a side path off that road to Stony Point, but was turned back by dense mountain laurel, brier bushes and a bog. You can also see the remains of a cement foundation for a seaplane hangar along that road, as well as a short channel that was dug to enter the secluded cove.

We passed up that walk and stayed right on the road to stick to our mission: to see if the ospreys had returned on their annual migration after spending the winter in Central and South America.

We hiked up a short hill to the highest point (182 feet) of the 3,349-acre preserve and then walked down the other side by a field. The road led to the southern tip of the Great Swamp, which the state acquired in 1950.

Along the path, a walker was sitting by a telephone pole in a natural stone chair, peering through binoculars and searching the swamp. He reported that he had spotted an osprey.

We saw one too, soaring high in the clouds and far in the distance. We decided to continue on the trail to try to get a closer look.

The road runs across the top of a mile-long dike that circles half the swamp and was built in the 1950s to create a wildlife marsh. Along the curving impoundment, jungle-like growth and the headwaters of the Pawcatuck River, including Chickasheen Brook, lie to the west. The expansive 138-acre swamp is to the east.

We passed a water depth gauge just off the bank and a circular steel and aluminum structure that may have included an underground gate to control the water levels. I've seen DEM workers driving along the impoundment to patrol the area in the past.

Just off the path, several ducks swam in the shallow water.

The trail took us under a long, straight line of transmission towers that carry power lines over the swamp and stretch far to the northeast and southwest.

Two rows of rotted pilings in the water once supported a boardwalk that ran out to the power lines in the swamp, but the wood is long gone.

We spotted the remains of an old osprey nest, built of sticks, twigs and grasses, on a tower about 50 yards offshore and a bulky nest on a tower south of the dike.

Ospreys migrate north each spring after spending the winter in South America and some of them make their nests atop transmission towers that run across the Great Swamp.

But the real attraction was on top of another tower 150 yards offshore, where we spotted two ospreys in a large, 3-foot nest in the middle of a horizontal plank on top of the towers. The ospreys return each spring to breed, and they stay until August.

While we watched, the fish-eating hawks took off and flew high over the west side of the swamp, staying far away from us. We could see that the ospreys have dark brown feathers on their back, and white below. The head is white with a dark face stripe. They can weigh 3 to 4 pounds and their wingspan can reach up to 6 feet.

The ospreys once faced extinction and from 1940 to 1970 the number of active nests between New York City and Boston decreased by 85 percent. A count in Rhode Island in 1967 found only a few nests.

But after ospreys were placed on the endangered species list and DDT and other pesticides were banned, their population grew, and reports show that there are now more than 150 nests in the state.

I've seen osprey nests on hikes at Osamequin Nature Preserve in

Barrington and Napatree Point in Westerly. Other hikers have recently reported that ospreys have returned to nests on the Narrow River.

After studying the flight of the two ospreys, we continued along the dike, which bent to the north. All the land in and around the swamp was once inhabited by Native Americans. The site of the Great Swamp Massacre, where fighters from several colonies killed many Narragansetts in December 1675 during King Philip's War, is just to the west on the other side of the railroad tracks.

We continued along the dike and walked carefully around two turtles sunning on the dry path. Just off the bank, we inspected several large beaver lodges built of branches, twigs, and mud. Several wood duck boxes stood on posts in the water. We noted two tube-like canisters near the top of telephone poles that lined the dike and wondered if they might be bat boxes.

The road led to the end of the swamp and ran up a short hill, under the power lines and to the junction where we had seen the Mulleedy marker on the way in. We passed a solo hiker in an orange vest who said he had been to the Saugatucket River that morning and watched ospreys spearing herring. He was now headed for a look at the ospreys at Great Swamp. From there, it was just a short walk to where we had parked.

There are many unique sightings on the trails in Rhode Island. But one of the most fascinating is the ospreys and their nests at Great Swamp. It's always encouraging to me that they return every spring. And it seems that if they can make the long flight back every April, I should be able to take a short walk to revisit them every year.

13   Black Farm

A Civil War grave gives hikers plenty to reflect on

Distance: 4 miles
Time: 2.5 hours
Difficulty: Easy on flat, well-marked trails

Access: Off Route 95, take Exit 4 and drive south on Woodville Alton Road to a parking lot on the left.
Parking: Available at a small lot
Dogs: Allowed, but must be leashed
Last Date Hiked: May 2022
Trailhead GPS: 41.46754, -71.72841

HOPKINTON—Charles Collins joined the Union Army during the Civil War and died at age 16 on the Mississippi River in 1863. He's buried next to his parents in a cemetery on farmland here where he grew up.

I paused at Collins' grave and thought about the tragic loss of life during a recent walk through the Black Farm Management Area. If you like history, there's a lot more to learn in the preserve, as well as several natural features to study.

The trails cross two bridges over Canonchet Book, half-circle a kettle pond, pass a curious stone foundation and follow an abandoned railroad bed to the Wood River, where stone abutments that once supported the tracks still stand.

Black Farm is only 245 acres, much smaller than other state management areas such as Arcadia and Buck Hill. But sometimes, smaller is better. It encourages you to stop more often and focus on what you see and hear. And there's a lot to think about at Black Farm.

From the trailhead, a friend and I set out on a section of the yellow-blazed Narragansett Trail, which runs for 22 miles through southern Rhode Island and Connecticut.

The footpath runs up a small rise and along a ridgeline with a shallow hollow below. At a fork, we walked left down the hillside and heard the

The graves of Charles Collins, a 16-year-old who died during the Civil War, and other members of the Collins family can be found in a stone wall-lined cemetery.

fast-rushing Canonchet Brook running through the valley well before we saw it.

The 15-foot-wide brook is crossed by a rickety bridge built of wooden slats nailed to thick tree branches. White water tumbled over mini waterfalls upstream. We studied the safety of the crossing, noted that somebody had replaced some of the boards to cover holes in the bridge and then walked across without incident.

On the other side, we hiked up a rise and through the trees got a first glimpse of Plain Pond, a circle-shaped body of water called a kettle pond. The basin was formed during the Ice Age when a large chunk of stagnant ice detached from a glacier and became partially buried in sediment. The slowly melting ice left behind the depression.

Plain Pond has no feeder streams and fills from groundwater and runoff. Its green tint is caused by reflections from the tall pines lining the banks.

From there, we took a left and hiked along an unremarkable trail through the woods until we reached the property boundary. We turned around

Black Farm

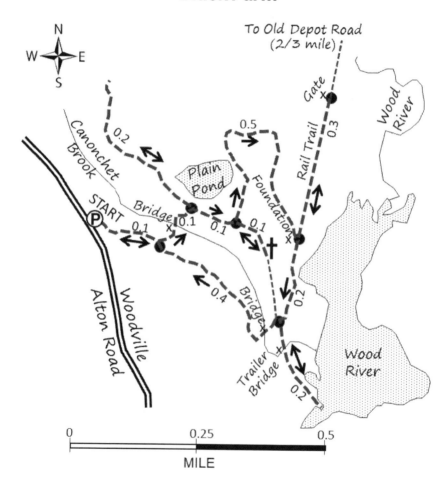

and walked by the pond on the left and continued until we saw a neat, rectangular-shaped, stone slab-lined cemetery, with a huge pine tree in the middle. It had been recently raked and cleared of brush.

We walked through an old iron gate and counted about 20 slate, granite, and marble headstones. One was marked for Thankful Collins Kenyon (1795-1890). The other side of the plot had other stones for more members of the Collins family, including one with an American flag and marked Charles L. Collins (1847-1863). After enlisting at age 15, Charles served in the Navy during the Civil War as a signal quartermaster and died suddenly of diphtheria a year later, far from home on board the steamer USS Eastport on the Mississippi River. His stone is inscribed:

"Dear Friends, my country calls me and I must go

With leaden wings to face the foe

And should I die on southern shore

I hope we'll meet to part no more."

The two graves next to Charles' are marked for his father, Charles Willet Collins (1813-1888) and his mother, Mary N. Hoxie Collins (1827-1908).

The Collins family owned and farmed the land for centuries, starting in 1710 when John Collins, a Quaker from Westerly, acquired 450 acres along the Wood River, part of 3,000 acres purchased by Collins and six others at the same time.

The land was passed down from fathers to sons, grandsons, and other relatives. At various periods over 200 years, the land was used for dairy, sheep and poultry farming and planted with orchards. For a time, lumber was harvested there.

The property was once called the Isaac Collins farm, named for a doctor who practiced in Richmond. He, his wife, Mary, and their children are buried in the cemetery.

After a series of land transfers, Margaret McCormack Black acquired the property in 1964. The Black family sold the land to the state in 1991 to be used as open space.

We stood quietly and respectfully by the graves for a few minutes before returning to the trail, heading back to the pond and walking along the banks through the woods.

The path broke right and descended a long slope before reaching an

A wooden slat bridge crosses the tumbling waters of the Canonchet Brook as it runs through the Black Farm Management Area.

unusual stone foundation. The granite block walls were about 5 feet high with three openings and two stone pillars at the far end in front of another chamber. But what caught my interest was the rounded corners of the walls.

Most of the old farm foundations for houses, cellar holes, barns, and storage sheds that I've seen on my hikes have squared-off corners. Some hikers think the structure may have been an old mill, but there was no stream or millrace nearby. Others said it was a depot or storage barn for a nearby railroad line.

I learned later that it was probably an ice house used to store blocks cut from Plain Pond. The ice may have been shipped on the freight line.

After inspecting the site, we picked up the trail that ran along a raised, straight-as-an arrow railroad bed that passed through a tunnel of pine trees.

We followed it north through a gate and then all the way to Old Depot Road. Side trails on the right lead to the Wood River.

Turning around, we retraced our steps by the stone foundation, skirted two fields and followed a path over a bridge made from a flat, low-bed trailer—with tires still attached—on stone pilings over a stream. We pondered how it was dropped into place, and then continued to the Wood River.

Stone pillars in the water once supported tracks for the Wood River Branch Railroad, which started running in 1874 and carried freight and passengers from a depot in Hope Valley to the Richmond Switch. A grain mill operator in Hope Valley bought the railroad in 1937. But it was abandoned after a grain elevator burned down in 1947. The tracks are gone now. We stood on a high, stone abutment on the river's edge and watched a beaver swim upstream.

After our break, we walked back over the trailer bridge and then took a left across a wooden bridge over Canonchet Brook. The stream was much wider here and running more slowly than it was at the section we crossed on the rickety bridge when we started. Several turtles sunned themselves on branches in the brook and plopped into the water as we passed.

The trail rimmed a field, with farm buildings and a barn on the left, before crossing a stone wall and entering the woods. We climbed a small hill and followed the path back to where we'd started.

Sometimes, hikes can be lively and a chance to swap stories with hiking buddies. Sometimes, the pace is fast to cover a lot of ground in a big preserve. And sometimes, walks are quiet and a time to reflect. Our hike through Black Farm was mostly like that, and I think visiting young Charles' grave had something to do with it.

A unique arched bridge with fitted dry stones crosses Borden Brook and connects with an old sawmill in Tiverton's Weetamoo Woods.

The Pardon Gray cemetery has been restored in the middle of a hayfield in the northwest section of the preserve.

14 Weetamoo Woods/Pardon Gray

On the trail of two historic figures in Tiverton

Distance: 6 miles
Time: 3 hours
Difficulty: Easy to moderate

Access: Follow Route 77 south. At the village of Tiverton, drive 3.2 miles south, and the Pardon Gray Preserve trailhead is on the left.
Parking: Available in a large gravel lot
Dogs: Allowed, but must be leashed or under voice command
Last Date Hiked: April 2023
Trailhead GPS: 41.59152, -71.19372

TIVERTON—Weetamoo Woods and Pardon Gray Preserve, two adjacent properties with miles of public trails over ridges and through an oak holly forest that surrounds a cedar swamp, are both named for historic figures.

Weetamoo was the last sachem of the Pocasset Wampanoag Tribe that sheltered for the winter on the land. She fought the Colonists in King Philip's War (1675-1676) and, after a defeat in battle, died while fleeing.

Pardon Gray, an 18th-century farmer and officer in the Revolutionary War, lived on the land and is buried in a family cemetery in the middle of a hayfield.

The huge preserves contain much more history, including the remains of a commercial sawmill with a unique arched bridge and an old road, measured in rods, that was once planned as the main route from Tiverton to Plymouth Colony.

I set out from the trailhead at the Pardon Gray Preserve in the northwest corner of the property and spotted a graveyard just to the south. I followed tractor tracks through a field to a restored, fieldstone-walled cemetery under shady, tall trees. The headstones dated to the 1700s. One is for Col. Pardon Gray, who was commissioned to supply the Continental Army's forces, which were garrisoned at nearby Fort Barton and defended the East Bay from the British.

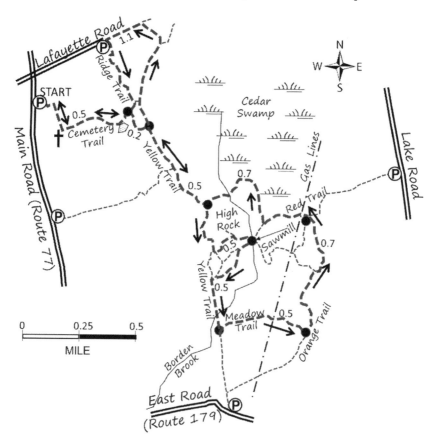

From there, I took the cemetery trail down the hillside, crossed Quaker Creek, passed a vernal pool and entered the dense Weetamoo Woods on a narrow path. The trail meandered up and then down a section of the lengthy Pocasset Ridge before reaching a yellow-blazed trail, the main path running north and south through the preserve.

I turned south, climbed over a couple of downed trees and reached the blue-blazed trail on the left. I took it east and found a side trail that climbed to the top of High Rock, with the Sakonnet River to the west.

Retracing my steps, I followed the blue-blazed trail to a highlight of the preserve—large, granite blocks that once formed a dam, foundation and millrace for a sawmill. Actually, there may have been two sawmills on the site: one from the late 1700s and another, larger commercial mill that operated in the mid-1800s and used iron turbines to power "up and down" reciprocating saws. The turbine chamber walls are still intact, as are inlet and outlet openings.

Even more interesting, just downstream is an arched bridge over Borden Brook that was built with dry, fitted stones. Most bridges for small farm or village sawmills were constructed with stone slabs. But the bridge here is about 15 feet wide and sturdy enough to carry wagons loaded with lumber.

I rested at the bridge, ate a snack and thought about the impact of the mill on jobs and the development of the local economy.

When I was done, I took the red-blazed trail to pick up the yellow trail again. I headed south, noting small cellar holes just off the path that may have been for mill workers' cabins. I passed private property on the right where a herd of cows grazed behind a barbed wire fence and stared at me as I walked by.

The path, lined with stone walls, widened. I learned later that Plymouth Colony in Massachusetts once controlled the land in the northern Sakonnet area and set aside lots for settlements as part of the Pocasset Purchase of 1681.

The trail I walked on was a segment of Eight Rod Road on the east boundary of the Pocasset Purchase and planned to connect Tiverton and Plymouth Colony. But the road to the north was never completed. (A rod equals 16.5 feet, so Eight Rod Road was 132 feet wide.)

Further down the road, I found a stone slab bridge over a narrower part of Borden Brook. Lumber wagons from the mill crossed the bridge and traveled down a section strengthened with fieldstones to a lumberyard and wharf on the Sakonnet River.

Just ahead, the Meadow Trail opened on the left. I walked by an old cement post, perhaps for a gate, and walked along the edge of a 12-acre field with rock outcroppings on the far side. A sign said that a habitat protection project was conducted to upgrade the meadow's condition for threatened grassland birds such as American kestrels and grasshopper sparrows.

The trail led to an orange-blazed path north and then to an intersection with the red trail, which I took west. At the next junction, I turned right on the green trail to loop back to the yellow trail.

I walked north along the edge of Cedar Swamp, including stands of Atlantic white cedar trees. Weetamoo, whose name means "speak to them," may have once hidden from the colonists in the swamp, which is surrounded by a rare oak and holly forest found in some coastal areas of southern New England.

The yellow trail ran to Lafayette Road, named for the Marquis de Lafayette, the Revolutionary War general who once stayed for a short time at a nearby house. I walked left on the road to a small parking lot and took the Ridge Trail south to return to the Pardon Gray cemetery, where I'd started.

Before I left, I sat on a 4-foot wall in the shady cemetery and thought about the fascinating history of the 655-acre Weetamoo Woods and 230-acre Pardon Gray Preserve. Besides a look into the past, the miles of trails offer many natural features, a pleasant walk and as much exercise as you want.

15   Vin Gormley Trail

The woods that transformed a city slicker

Distance: 8.2 miles
Time: 4 hours
Difficulty: Easy to moderate

Access: Off Route 1 southbound, take Prosser Road for 0.6 miles to the Burlingame Picnic Area on the left.
Parking: Available at a parking lot
Dogs: Allowed, but must be leashed
Last Date Hiked: April 2022
Trailhead GPS: 41.38038, -71.67725

CHARLESTOWN—John Vincent "Vin" Gormley spent hundreds of hours clearing, blazing and maintaining trails in the Arcadia Management Area and Burlingame State Park until he was well into his 80s.

Side spurs from the Vin Gormley Trail lead to great views of the 573-acre Watchaug Pond.

Vin Gormley Trail

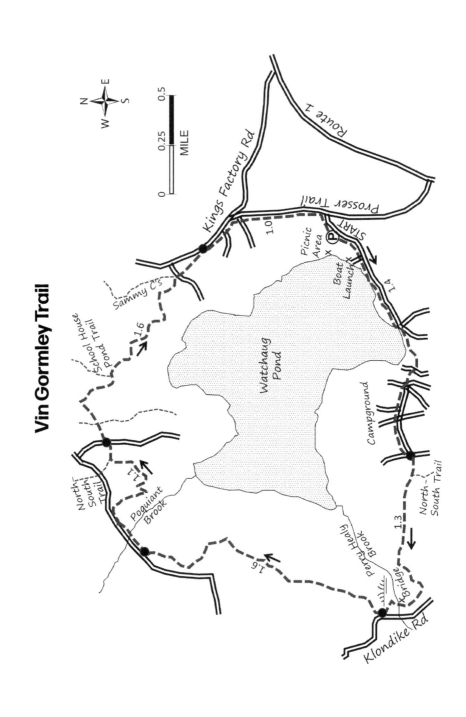

A wooden boardwalk meanders over a swampy section of the Vin Gormley Trail.

When a trail around Watchaug Pond was renamed in his honor in 1991, Gormley said he started out as a "city slicker" but "Once I got into the woods, I was sold." So have a lot of other hikers who followed his paths. I'm one of them.

A friend and I set out on the 8.2-mile loop from the Burlingame Picnic Area off Prosser Road, just above the beach on the eastern shore of Watchaug Pond. The yellow-blazed trail starts on a dirt road with houses on the left. Just ahead on the right is the Barton Hurley Boat Launch, named for the veteran and conservationist from Charlestown.

Several side spurs lead to the shore and panoramic views of the 900-acre pond. The trail ducks into the woods on a well-trod footpath and enters the 29-acre Kimball Wildlife Refuge, owned by the Rhode Island Department of Environmental Management, and a popular spot for birders.

After a bit, we crossed into the Burlingame Camping Area between the camp store and a playground. The cabins and campsites were empty, but two workers were spreading mulch and gravel to get ready for another camping season.

The trail cuts across the campground, passes a road to the beach on the right and then leads to a kiosk with a map and a short biography of Gormley. I learned that he had served in the Civilian Conservation Corps and worked in naval shipyards in California during World War II. He later lived in Cranston, attended St. Mark's Church, and worked for the state as a carpenter before retiring in 1989, having never missed a day of work.

Gormley also volunteered on the Trails Committee of the Appalachian Mountain Club. He spent years on the trails around Watchaug Pond, cutting back growth, picking up trash and retracing blazes. In September 1991, the Rhode Island House of Representatives passed a special act that renamed the yellow trail for Gormley. In an interview, he said, "Once you get out in the woods, you never forget them. It's so peaceful." Gormley died in 2000 at the age of 89.

I thought about Gormley while continuing down a lovely, wooded lane under oak and maple trees, with a few holly trees mixed in, before entering a section of dense, damp forest. The blue-blazed North South Trail, which runs 78 miles from Charlestown to Burrillville, enters from the left and merges with the yellow-blazed trail.

After crossing several stone walls, the path's terrain becomes swampy and covered in ferns. In the summer, insects swarm the area.

The trail here was originally cut by the Youth Conservation Corps for the DEM in 1960. Starting in the 1980s, Gormley upgraded the path by cutting diseased pine trees, loading the 12-foot sections into his trailer, and hauling them to the low areas. After stripping the logs of their bark, he used them to build 600 feet of bog bridges over the wetlands.

During the following decades, some of the bridges were replaced by 4-foot-wide wooden-board walkways that meander above the lowlands. AMC volunteers gather every September in Gormley's memory to brush the trails, and many of the bridges are now carved with "AMC" and the year they were installed.

The trail continues through the woods and crosses the Perry Healy Brook over a small, neat, covered bridge named for Gormley. We rested on benches inside the latticed-sided bridge and listened to the clacking of the first wood frogs of the season.

After our break, we walked on the trail to Buckeye Brook Road, took

The covered bridge over the Perry Healy Brook is named for John Vincent "Vin" Gormley, a veteran and conservationist from Charlestown.

a right for about a hundred yards, reentered the woods, and followed the path until we reached the road again. We turned right on the road, crossed a bridge over Poquiant Brook and then walked back into the woods at a sign on the right for the yellow-blazed trail.

The second half of the Gormley Trail is quite different from the first half and runs far away from the pond. Starting under a beech grove, the rocky and rooted trail runs across ridges, along the base of cliffs and by sharp glacial rocks.

One section passes through a tunnel of mountain laurel while others follow old farm lanes. Small seasonal streams cross the path in places and flow downhill toward the pond, which isn't visible from the trail. We crossed bridges over some brooks and rock-hopped over others. A couple of mini waterfalls tumble over flat, smooth stony areas. Several side trails and roads break off the path, but the yellow blazes are easy to follow.

At one point, after staying together for about 4 miles, the North South Trail splits off from the yellow-blazed trail and heads north. We continued east on the yellow-blazed trail and noted signs for side spurs for the School House Pond Preserve and Sammy C's trail. The path exits the woods, crosses a road, and runs uphill to Kings Factory Road. We turned right and passed some houses and a youth camp to reach Prosser Trail. We followed it back to where we'd started.

At the ribbon cutting for the Gormley Trail, Gormley talked about the work he had put in, but added, "If I live to be 100, I won't have that trail the way it should be."

Not true, Vin. And thousands of hikers thank you for a job well done.

16 Trustom Pond

In the silence of the sanctuary, hikers and migratory birds find solace

Distance: 3 miles
Time: 2 hours
Difficulty: Easy on flat paths

Access: Take Route 1 to Moonstone Beach Road. Drive south and take a right on Matunuck School House Road to the refuge entrance.
Parking: Available in two lots at the trailhead
Dogs: Not allowed
Last Date Hiked: October 2021
Trailhead GPS: 41.38394, -71.58574

SOUTH KINGSTOWN—Two birders, as still as stone, peered through binoculars at a gulp of cormorants perched on a rock in the middle of the pond.

Farther out, a photographer, with his back to the sun rising in the east, set up a tripod on a barrier beach to capture a shot of some pied-billed grebes.

And still more distant on the horizon, sailboats, tankers, and ferries cruised on Block Island Sound.

All of this occurred in almost total silence, broken only by the sound of black ducks flapping to dry their feathers after diving for breakfast or the occasional far-away drone of a ferry's diesel engine.

Trustom Pond is special—not only for its sights and sounds, but because the sanctuary's walkers respect the land and fellow hikers.

They nod slightly as they pass one another or offer a quiet, "Morning." One young man coming from the opposite direction stepped off a narrow path to let me pass. When I interrupted the birders to ask if they knew the location of an old windmill on the property, they patiently explained in great detail how to get there.

It was much appreciated.

The 787-acre national wildlife preserve was once part of a coastal sheep farm run by the Morse family. A plaque on a rock at the trailhead notes

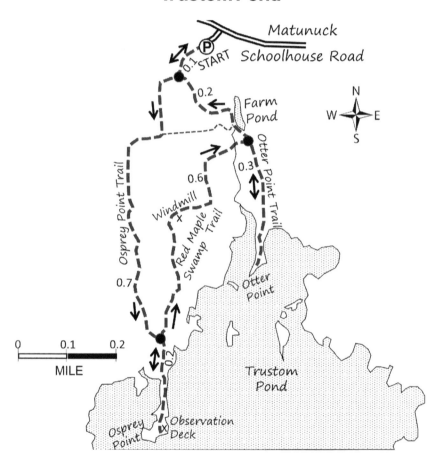

Trustom Pond glimmers in the early morning light. The national wildlife refuge in South Kingstown is a haven for a wide variety of birds and animals.

that after the death of Alfred Hudson Morse, his widow, Ann Kenyon Morse, donated 365 acres to the U.S. Fish and Wildlife Service in 1974, establishing Trustom Pond National Wildlife Refuge. In 1982, the Audubon Society donated an additional 115 acres of barrier beach habitat, a nesting area on the southern boundary of the preserve for the least tern and the piping plover.

The preserve serves an important purpose. Trustom Pond is the only undeveloped coastal salt pond in Rhode Island and has become a sanctuary to many species of wildlife during various migratory seasons.

Walkers have identified 300 species of birds, 40 mammals and 20 species of reptiles and amphibians in the fields, shrublands, woodlands, low-lying marshes, fresh and saltwater ponds, sandy beaches, and dunes.

On a recent walk to the pond, I set out alone from an information kiosk and passed through a thicket filled with bird sounds. I soon reached a Y-intersection facing a huge, tall grass field that was once a hayfield for the sheep farm and has since been converted to native warm-season grasses,

Just off the path to Osprey Point, a deer pauses from nibbling leaves wet with the morning dew.

including little and big blue stem, switch grass, and Indian grass. The field attracts bobolinks, northern harriers, Eastern bluebirds, and many other types of birds.

I half-circled the field and passed a sitting bench before ducking into the woods on a wide, winding road. Just ahead, I interrupted a deer nibbling on some leaves still wet with the morning dew. We stared at each other for a few minutes before I moved on.

A short distance later, a path opened on the left, but I stayed right and walked to two observation decks that look out on Trustom Pond.

A white mute swan swims just offshore in Trustom Pond.

At the second platform, the two birders I mentioned earlier were studying the cormorants. After they left, I lingered for quite a while and watched a white mute swan swim along the banks and duck its long neck and orange bill in the water for food.

I noted the sandy Moonstone barrier beach on the far, southern side of the pond as a slight sea breeze picked up.

Retracing my steps, I returned to the intersection and this time went right on the Red Maple Swamp trail through the woods. Some of the abandoned sheep pastures have been reclaimed by the forest.

After about a half mile, at a bench, I took a side path (following the good directions provided by the birders) to find the overgrown metal frame of a 25-foot-tall windmill with a rusty fan wheel at the top that no longer turns in the wind. A circular, cement-lined well at the base collected water pumped by the windmill for the sheep. The wooden troughs where they drank are long gone.

So is the sheep shed back up the path. Stone walls running through the dense brush once marked the pastures and cart paths.

I returned to the main trail, headed north to another junction, and turned right on a path lined with fragrant wild berry bushes. Fields and private property were marked on the left, and the Morses once used a cabin on the right as a retreat.

The path continued on a peninsula to Otter Point. From another observation deck, you can see an osprey nest, an island, the pond and the ocean and blue sky far beyond.

I found a short path to a clearing at the point, with an unobstructed view of water on three sides. There was a chain around a tree that was probably used to tie up a boat.

I retraced my steps to the intersection and turned right. With the huge field to my left, I walked down a side path to a still, man-made farm pond, covered with lily pads. After watching the birds for a while, it was time to head back on a wide, winding path through the open fields to the trailhead.

Trustom Pond is always changing with the seasons, the migratory patterns of the birds and the growth of the fields and vegetation. But I hope the coastal sanctuary always stays quiet, peaceful, and welcoming.

17 Francis C. Carter Memorial Preserve

Signs of returning life at a moth-ravaged preserve

Distance: 5.6 miles
Time: 3 hours
Difficulty: Easy on flat paths with moderate climbs on rocky ridges

Access: From Route 95, take Route 138 east. Turn onto Route 112 south and drive four miles to the trailhead on the right.
Parking: Available at a parking lot
Dogs: Allowed, but must be leashed
Last Date Hiked: March 2022
Trailhead GPS: 41.43893, -71.65673

CHARLESTOWN—One path, covered with a soft carpet of pine needles, runs through a forest of tall Eastern white pines. Another trail circles a huge, open grassland. And a third crosses the Charlestown Moraine—a long ridgeline created 12,000 years ago when the edge of a glacier paused in its retreat and deposited rock and sediment.

The variety of trails and the natural beauty of the Francis C. Carter Memorial Preserve caught my attention during an early-morning winter walk.

I also was stunned to see acres of dead, defoliated oak trees.

I had read about an infestation of spongy moth caterpillars (formerly known as gypsy moths) several years ago but was shocked to see the extent of the devastation and wondered how, and if, the forest would ever come back.

The defoliation is in the eastern section of the 1,100-acre preserve, one of the largest in the state, established in 2001 by The Nature Conservancy, a nonprofit environmental organization.

The preserve is named for Francis "Frank" Carter, the late outdoorsman and former head of the Champlin Foundation who formed a partnership with The Nature Conservancy to conserve and protect land for the public.

Setting out from a trailhead off Carolina Back Road (Route 112), my

Francis C. Carter Memorial Preserve

A stone-and-earthen dam may have once been the site of a water-powered shingle mill in the 1800s.

friend George and I passed a sign warning of falling branches from the dead oaks.

Just off the start of the trail, we studied a vernal pool—a shallow seasonal pool of water that in a month or so will spring to life with wood frogs and salamanders that return there to breed and grow.

The orange-blazed trail, alternately muddy or frozen in spots, climbs along ledges and by outcroppings that form the long moraine.

When we reached the top of a hill, we saw the damage from the spongy moth caterpillar infestation and drought in 2016 and 2017 that killed 240 acres of oak forest. Long stretches of dead, standing trees appear across the ridge.

Large snags of fallen dead oaks lay just off the path. Some cover sections of stone walls.

I learned later that there are no plans for any planting or timber-salvaging operations on the land. Eventually, over decades, the forest will regenerate, but perhaps this time with a mix of oak, white pine, or pitch

A straight, pine needle-covered path runs under Eastern white pine trees on the southern border of the Carter Memorial Preserve.

pine, depending on what type of seeds blow in, according to Tim Mooney, a former preserve manager at Carter and now the marketing and communications manager for the Rhode Island chapter of The Nature Conservancy.

With the lack of a heavy tree canopy, more sunlight is reaching the forest floor, which is now transitioning to shrubs or "early successional" growth of blueberry and huckleberry. Later, wild black cherry and gray birch will take root.

The shift is also creating additional habitat for declining populations of shrub-nesting songbirds such as prairie warblers, blue-winged warblers and indigo buntings, Mooney said. The birds usually nest around the edges of the preserve's field but are now showing up in the upland sections. The standing dead trees attract woodpeckers and hawks, and the larger oaks will become "den trees" for small mammals.

After studying the scarred forest, we continued down the hillside and crossed an earth and stone dam over a trickling stream. Nearby were stone walls, a cart path, and a small pond. The site may have been on property once owned by Benjamin Tucker (1804-1890), who ran Tucker's Shingle Mill, a water-powered mill.

We picked up the blue-blazed trail that rose to high ground, giving us a look north to a frozen pond where ice blocks once were cut for refrigeration.

The level of the water rises and falls with beaver activity, and the outflow drains under railroad tracks to the Pawcatuck River. While we were studying the pond, an Amtrak train whooshed through the trees in the distance.

From the blue-blazed trail, we took a yellow-blazed trail that was once a sheep path and that opens to a 60-acre grassland, one of the largest managed for wildlife in the state. Once a potato field in the 1970s, the grassland is mowed annually by workers for the Audubon Society of Rhode Island under contract with The Nature Conservancy.

The grassland provides habitat for pollinators and birds, including woodcocks, kestrels, and tree swallows, and is one of two nesting areas for grasshopper sparrows in Rhode Island. The other is on Block Island.

We circled the field and picked up a red-blazed trail. Another path breaks off to the east and passes under a pitch pine and hardwood forest along the Pawcatuck River before reaching a trailhead at King's Factory Road. The area was once owned by United Nuclear, a nuclear fuel recovery plant. After the plant closed in the 1980s, the federal government declared the land a Superfund site and began a 30-year cleanup.

We decided to save that path for another day, though, and continued on the red-blazed trail, which in places is called the Narragansett Loop. For a long stretch, the path runs straight as an arrow under Eastern white pines.

At a junction, we turned north and passed through a boulder field and then by an old fireplace that may have been part of a family camp, now long gone.

Along the trail, we noted small educational signs pointing out types of trees in that section of the forest: red cedar, mockernut hickory, sassafras, black birch, and witch hazel.

The path then follows a road to another trailhead off Old Mill Road before heading back along the blue-blazed trail to the moraine, where you can see more evidence of the spongy moth devastation. The trail crossed the ridge and returned us to where we'd started.

In all, we hiked 5.6 miles on four interconnected, color-coded trails.

Most of the preserve was not damaged by the spongy moths, and the effort years ago to acquire and protect a large tract of land helped make the forest more resilient to natural disasters and better able to regenerate. The scars will heal at Carter, and new trees will grow strong again.

18 Fisherville Brook Wildlife Refuge

Where birds, beavers and minks make their homes

Distance: 4.2 miles
Time: 2 hours
Difficulty: Easy to moderate

Access: From Route 102, take Widow Sweets Road at the intersection near Exeter Town Hall. Drive 0.4 miles and turn right on Pardon Joslin Road for 0.7 miles to the parking lot on the right. The preserve is open from sunrise to sunset.
Parking: Available at a lot at the trailhead
Dogs: Not allowed
Last Date Hiked: June 2022
Trailhead GPS: 41.59040, -71.57038

EXETER—An old mill pond with a footbridge on one end above a beaver dam and a waterfall over a stone dam at the other are among the surprises at the Fisherville Brook Wildlife Refuge.

There is also a variety of birds to spot in a grassy, hillside pasture and, if you're lucky, you may discover a mink by the water and streams. (I saw the birds but not the mink.)

You also have several choices of trails.

One circles Upper Pond on the southern side of the 1,010-acre preserve managed by the Audubon Society of Rhode Island. It's perfect for families and first-time hikers. There's another loop trail on the northern side of the refuge that's a bit more rugged and runs by ridges, small hills, brooks and huge glacial erratics left from the Ice Age.

I set out from the parking lot and stopped at a kiosk to check the map. I studied the color-coded trails, took a cellphone picture, and chose the blue-blazed path headed south.

The wide trail rises and falls over small ridges and below tall white pine trees. At a junction with the yellow-blazed trail, I took the short loop along the edge of a white cedar swamp before returning to the blue-blazed trail.

A little further down the path, there's a bench and a short side spur on

Fisherville Brook Wildlife Refuge

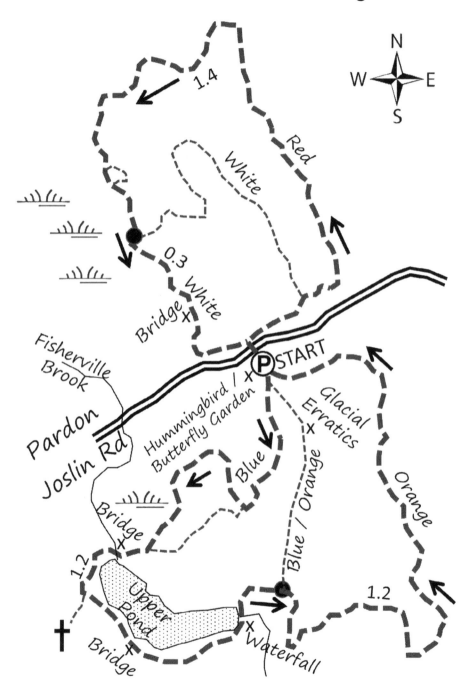

the left to a flat ledge where I've seen families pause for a break and look down the slope at the small, L-shaped mill pond.

After a gentle descent, you'll come to a wooden footbridge over Fisherville Brook, which feeds the pond from the north. If you look down, you'll see the beaver activity that has blocked some of the water flow into the pond and created a large swampy area upstream. And don't miss the tree gnawed almost all the way through at the start of the bridge.

Trail stewards periodically clear out the branches and mud dams built by the beavers that sometimes flood the trails. Beavers are most active in the fall, when they construct dams to raise the water level before winter so they can get to their food storage under the ice.

Hikers report seeing or hearing otters, muskrats, fox, deer, wood frogs, spring peepers and minks. I was especially interested in the minks, which have long, skinny chocolate-brown bodies and live near water, where they dig burrows in riverbanks or use old muskrat or beaver dens. They eat muskrats, frogs, fish, and other small animals. But I didn't see one on this walk.

On the far side of the bridge, the trail skirts the lily-pad-covered Upper Pond, with several pastures on a hillside on the right, and several lean-tos built with thick branches under pine trees at the shoreline.

A sign marks a side trail for a short walk up a hill on the right to a large, grassy field. A sign says it is mowed once a year in the fall to preserve the mix of grasses and forbs (herbaceous flowering plants) that are a natural habitat for plants and grassland animals. Without regular mowing, the fields would revert to forest land and be dominated in 15 or 20 years by shrubs and trees.

In the middle of the meadow is a raised, stone-wall-lined graveyard on land that was once the old John Gardner (1754-1837) homestead and later the Reuben Brown farm. The headstones mark graves from the 1800s and 1900s for members of the Gardner, Sweet, Bailey, and Hall families.

The graveyard is encircled with nesting boxes of various shapes and heights with different-sized holes to attract a variety of birds, said Laura Carberry, refuge manager. The small wooden boxes are home to tree swallows and bluebirds. I took some time to watch a small tree swallow with blue feathers perched on top of one.

An odd-shaped structure, called a gourd, with bulbous white boxes arranged in a ring at the top of a tall pole is for purple martins, which like to live in a community. A nesting pair had settled in one of the gourds.

Another tall pole with a box on top is for the American kestrel, the smallest of falcons, which like to live in cavities.

While watching the birds, I surveyed the pasture and the trees, including a few cedars, and the stone walls that surround it. A large farmhouse is about 400 feet higher up the hill. I heard a dog bark.

Returning to the blue-blazed trail, I continued on the path around the pond and walked over a lengthy set of bridges made from recycled plastic planks over lowlands that are dry now but sometimes flood from beaver activity and during rainy seasons.

Carberry said a woman from Exeter who loved the refuge donated the planks to extend an existing boardwalk. An Eagle Scout built the extension and, at the woman's request, put up a sign, so hikers and her grandchildren would know of their donation. It reads: "Donated by the grandchildren of the Levesque and LaBossiere families."

The trail skirts the pond before crossing a wooden bridge over a dam that forms a waterfall where outflow from the pond tumbles about eight feet to a spillway. The dam was built to create Upper Pond and includes a stone-block foundation and what looks like a sluice gate. I read that a sawmill and later a cotton spinning mill once operated there. During the winter, ice blocks were cut from the pond.

The water flows into Fisherville Brook, which runs south under Route 102 to merge with Sodom Brook before entering the Queen River. Along the way, it passes through Fisherville, once a small mill town that thrived in the mid-19th century. The remains, including a gristmill, sawmill, and a Cape-style house, were listed on the National Register of Historic Places in 1980.

The trail crossed the walkway over the dam and reached a junction in about 50 yards. The blue-blazed trail goes left and returns to the parking lot. I turned right on the orange-blazed trail, which crossed two small bridges over streams and passed under oak and beech trees and by several fields before returning to the lot where I'd started.

Walking north across Pardon Joslin Road, I set out for the second loop

Water from Upper Pond flows over a stone dam, once the site of a 19th-century mill, to form Fisherville Brook, which runs south to the Queen River.

The placid, L-shaped Upper Pond was created by building a dam on Fisherville Brook.

through the other half of the preserve. I walked a few yards up a driveway for a private residence and turned right on the red-blazed, pine-needle-covered trail that ran up a small hill. The woods here were dense and quiet.

There are several benches along the trail that passes through tunnels of mountain laurel. At the northern section of the path, I noted several cairns in no apparent order. I've seen those before in Exeter, Hopkinton, and Coventry. Historians say they may have been built from rocks cleared from fields by early settlers or by Native Americans for ceremonial purposes. Nobody's sure.

The trail turned south, and, at a bench, I went left on a short unmarked loop by a stone wall and some of the largest glacial erratics on the property. A hiker's report said a small, unmarked graveyard is nearby, but I couldn't find it. I did see what may be small kettle holes formed when indentations in the land filled with chunks of glacial ice that melted, creating the depressions.

I returned to the red-blazed trail. A white-blazed inner loop trail opened on the left, but I stayed straight, crossed a small bridge, and passed what looked like an old nature study course for children. I spotted a house and shed on the left before walking downhill and back to where I'd started.

Before you leave Fisherville, check out the Pollinator Garden just off the parking lot. It's planted with flowers and plants to attract and support pollinators, such as bees and butterflies, and curb the decline in their population.

19 Wolf Hill Forest Preserve

Discovering the woods' icy wonders on a winter day

Distance: 4 miles
Time: 3 hours
Difficulty: Easy to moderate on rocky ridges and hills

Access: Off Route 5 and 116, look for a sign for Autumn Run on Waterview Drive. Go 100 yards southeast to the entrance to the Smithfield Conservation Center on the right.
Parking: Available for 12 cars at the trailhead
Dogs: Allowed on a leash
Last Date Hiked: February 2021
Trailhead GPS: 41.89873, -71.53985

SMITHFIELD—Vernal pools—small, shallow depressions of fresh water—appear just off many of the trails in the Wolf Hill Forest Preserve. They are iced-over, quiet, lovely to look at and lifeless in the dead of winter.

But after the ground thaws, the pools will spring to life with wood frogs, salamanders and fairy shrimp that return to breed and grow. It happens every spring, even though the COVID-19 pandemic seems to have knocked the world out of balance.

The vernal pools are just one spot to pause and think in the preserve.

There's also a granite outcropping where a military plane crashed in 1943, killing three airmen, an outlook where scouts once camped and watched the distant lights of Providence, and a waterfall crusted with icicles that cling to the cliffs near an old quarry.

It's amazing what you can find and learn when you walk in the woods.

I set out from Stump Pond, off Waterview Drive and Routes 5 and 116, on a sunny, cold morning in February and listened for a few minutes to the booms from the expanding ice on the water.

There's an information kiosk and a walkway through a hole in a 10-foot hedge on the trail named for Leo Bouchard, who started the town's conservation commission.

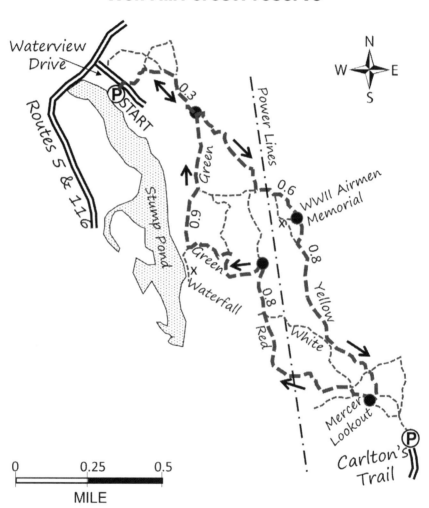

A vernal pool can be seen just off the yellow-blazed trail in the Wolf Hill Forest Preserve in Smithfield. In the spring, the shallow depression of water will fill with wood frogs, salamanders, and fairy shrimp.

The yellow-blazed trail follows a long, winding gradual incline, at times rocky and rooted. Just before the crest of a ridge, there's a tiny, frozen vernal pool. Somewhere on the hillside, toads are burrowed into the soil in the woodlands. When temperatures reach 50 degrees, they will make their way to the pools to breed.

The trail opens to a barren stretch under high-voltage transmission lines. You can see the long, rocky ridgeline running north and south that forms Wolf Hill, named for the old trail and road that once ran to Esmond until Route 295 blocked the way.

The yellow-blazed path leads back into the woods. Not far ahead, there's a sign for a loop to the World War II Airmen Memorial, a stone marker and plaque with American flags dedicated to 2nd Lt. Otis R. Portewig, of Richmond, Virginia; Tech. Sgt. Herbert Booth, of Rahway, New Jersey; and 2nd Lt. Saul Winsten, of Pawtucket. They perished on the rocky mound when the right engine failed on their twin-engine Lockheed B-34 and they

A waterfall tumbles 30 feet over dark green, mossy ledges and gray cliffs just off Mountaindale Road.

From the remains of a foundation and stone chimney, left from an abandoned Boy Scout camp, hikers can see downtown Providence and farther east to Narragansett Bay.

crashed, creating a 50-yard debris field. Hikers pay their respects and stack stones on a huge boulder there.

I continued on the yellow-blazed trail under oak, maple, pine and hemlock trees and around moss-covered boulders. That led to the white-blazed trail that crossed an intersection of dirt roads and side paths. From there, it's an easy walk to Mercer Lookout, a 450-foot overlook and the high point of the preserve.

There are remains of a cement foundation and stone chimney and fireplace from an abandoned Providence Boy Scout camp that burned in the 1940s or 1950s. Volunteers recently cleared trees and reclaimed a panoramic view to the east of downtown Providence and farther still to Narragansett Bay.

Hikers say sharp eyes can also see the Mount Hope Bridge, but not these old peepers.

There's a side trail to the right of the chimney that leads to a vernal pool with a granite bench and memorial to Tom Robitaille, a late member of the Smithfield Land Trust. It must be enjoyable to sit there in the spring and listen to life in the forest.

I retraced my steps, headed west on a side spur and reached the rim of 30-foot cliffs overlooking a large, closed quarry. There's graffiti on the ledges, and it's pretty dangerous in icy conditions. Be careful.

I headed back on the red-blazed Ken Weber Trail, named for the late naturalist, Smithfield resident and columnist for The Providence Journal.

There are several more vernal pools at the base of a long series of ledges that mark the top of the ridge. There's a small sign noting that spotted salamanders migrate to the pools on rainy nights to mate and breed. The fairy shrimp lay eggs on the bottom of the pools that stay there when the pools dry up in the summer and hatch later when the pools refill in the fall. It's simple but life-sustaining.

The Weber trail leads to the green-blazed trail named for Mary Mowry, a benefactor who donated land for the preserve. Some sections are steep, rocky, and challenging. A side trail west and down a slope opens to a wide road that runs alongside Stump Pond. I met two hikers who led me south along the road to a gate on Mountaindale Road. A path off to the left leads to private property (I didn't see any no-trespassing signs) and a gorgeous waterfall tumbling 30 feet over dark-green mossy ledges and gray cliffs, while forming long, white icicles. It was a nice respite after a full morning of hiking.

I returned to the road around Stump Pond and walked up the hill to the green-blazed trail, which led me back to the yellow-blazed trail and the lot where I'd parked.

The trails at Wolf Hill, some on old farm roads, are well-marked and color-coded. There are short and long loops over easy to moderate terrain, with some elevation changes. Take your time. There are plenty of places to stop and enjoy the natural scenery.

All morning, I saw only three hikers in the 300-acre preserve managed by the Smithfield Land Trust.

I made a note to come back in the spring. By then, I bet the vernal pools will be full of life and the trails will be busier with hikers emerging from a long, dark winter.

20 Fort Barton Woods

Today a peaceful preserve with a haunting legacy of Colonial violence

Distance: 3.5 miles
Time: 2 hours
Difficulty: Easy to moderate, with some rocky and rooted paths

Access: Off Route 77 (Main Road), take a left on Lawton Avenue to the top of the hill. The trailhead is at the intersection of Lawton Avenue and Highland Avenue.
Parking: Available at a paved lot across from Tiverton Town Hall
Dogs: Allowed, but must be leashed or under voice control and kept on the marked trails
Last Date Hiked: June 2022
Trailhead GPS: 41.62502, -71.20744.

TIVERTON—The Sin and Flesh Brook that winds through Fort Barton Woods is one of the most intriguing places I've ever come across while hiking in Rhode Island.

The origin of the name dates back 350 years to King Philip's War between the Colonists and Native Americans, a series of bloody battles marked by many atrocities.

In the deep woods here in 1676, Zoeth Howland, a Quaker preacher, was tortured and killed while traveling from his home in Dartmouth to visit a congregation in Newport. His mutilated body was found in an unnamed stream that became known as "Sinning Flesh River." Over the years, the name evolved to Sin and Flesh Brook.

That violent history contrasts with the quiet, peaceful preserve I found when I hiked through the 98-acre sanctuary. The brook meanders through the isolated eastern side of the preserve under a dense canopy of oaks, maples, and holly trees. Thick green ferns carpet the banks.

I set out to see the brook for myself early one foggy morning from the trailhead on the western side of the preserve, which is managed by the Tiverton Land Trust. I walked up a short, steep, paved pathway to the remains of fortified earthworks built on a granite outcropping on High

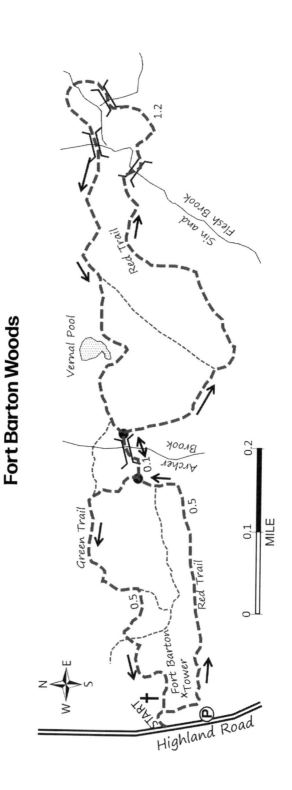

Hill during the Revolutionary War. The redoubt on a bluff 110 feet above the Sakonnet River defended the narrow passage between Tiverton and Portsmouth. From 1776 to 1779, it also served as a lookout to check on the British occupation of Aquidneck Island.

The high ground, once called Tiverton Heights, is now named in honor of Lt. Col. William Barton.

In 1777, Barton led a ragtag band of Colonists on a daring raid by boat around Prudence Island to Portsmouth. They rowed three boats in the dark of night through the British fleet, slipped ashore and captured British Gen. Richard Prescott in his quarters.

The raid had little strategic value, but word of Prescott being led off in his nightshirt swept through the Colonies and boosted the morale of the rebels.

A 20-story observation tower now stands on the high point next to a pole flying the American flag. I decided to save the climb to the top for later, after the fog had lifted.

From behind the tower, I walked down a gravel path to a set of wooden steps that led down a steep embankment and into Fort Barton Woods.

I picked up the red-blazed trail and passed by a farm behind a stone wall on the right, where I heard a rooster crow before seeing chickens in a pen pecking for food. The path, rocky and rooted in places, ran up and down a small ridge before crossing a wooden bridge over Archer Brook.

Continuing east under stands of holly, birch, and black cherry trees, I crossed a stone wall and passed through a muddy area before getting a first glimpse of Sin and Flesh Brook, which meandered easily through the woods.

The Pocassets, part of the Wampanoag nation, lived and hunted here for thousands of years. During King Philip's War (1675-1676), they joined other tribes to fight the Colonists after an escalating series of disputes over land claims, tribal rights, and cultural tensions. When the Colonists encroached on local lands, the Native Americans retaliated by raiding settlers' homes and property. That led to more brutal clashes.

Two of the first armed engagements of King Philip's War took place in Tiverton as the war spread throughout the region.

In December 1675, in what is now South Kingstown, the Colonists

Several wooden bridges cross the Sin and Flesh Brook as it meanders southwest through Fort Barton Woods.

massacred 600 Native Americans, including women and children, and burned dwellings and food in what came to be called the Great Swamp Massacre.

About 150 members of the Colonial militia died in the battle.

In response, the Native Americans burned settlements and killed Colonists throughout Rhode Island. In 1676, Howland, the preacher, was found dead in Sin and Flesh Brook. Historians have found court records that named a Native American as his killer.

The war lasted until Canonchet, chief of the Narragansetts, and later, Metacomet, chief of the Pokanoket and also known as King Philip, were killed.

As the war ended, the Pocassets were driven from the land, which was granted to Colonists, in some cases for outstanding service during the war. Their farms dominated Tiverton for hundreds of years. The stone walls that crisscross Fort Barton Woods were probably constructed as property lines or barriers to keep livestock from wandering into swampy areas.

A wooden tower was erected in 1970 on the site of fortified earthworks built by Colonial militia during the Revolutionary War.

I paused and thought about all that history as I followed the red-blazed trail across a wooden bridge over the Sin and Flesh Brook, which flows southwest into Nannaquaket Pond. I crossed the winding brook three more times on wide, wooden-board bridges. At one bend in the river, in a darkened area heavily shaded by tall oaks, the only sound was the water rippling over stones in the shallow stream. It felt a bit eerie.

The trail bent north and then east, with a stone wall running parallel to the path. I passed through a rocky area of outcroppings and boulders before dipping down to some wetlands, including a placid, vernal pool with red maple and yellow birch trees growing on a small island in the middle. I heard the strum, a deep, banjo-like twang, of a frog.

At a junction, a blue-blazed cross trail opened on the left, but I continued straight on the red-blazed trail. When I reached a green-blazed trail on the right, I took it up a hillside and through what's called Highland Woods.

From there, I took a short path on the left and found a small, stone-lined cemetery with stones for members of the Manchester and Durfee families.

Just a short walk up the hillside on the left was the observation tower I'd passed when I started. The weather had cleared, and I climbed the wooden tower, erected in 1970, for a panoramic view west to the Sakonnet Passage and Mount Hope Bay. I could see the Sakonnet River Bridge and Roger Williams University far in the distance.

The area around me had once been a staging ground for 11,000 Colonial troops who were ferried across the passage in 1778 to fight in the Battle of Rhode Island on Aquidneck Island. Their assault was unsuccessful.

When I was done studying the scene, I walked back down the hill to where I had started.

I was intrigued by what I had observed, though, and read some more research done by the Tiverton Historical Society into the meaning of Sinning Flesh River that later became Sin and Flesh Brook. Nobody really knows what the name means. I did learn that Howland became a Quaker after speaking out publicly and harshly against the Puritans, whose clergy fined him, put him in the stocks and drove him from his home in Plymouth.

Historians ponder whether the name refers to a sinful man who was punished for his beliefs? Or is it as simple as the sinful murder of a peaceful preacher?

Or does it mean something else altogether? Whatever the derivation, the name, and its history, are haunting and not easy to forget.

Urban Walks

Stone steps built by the Works Progress Administration in the 1930s climb to a road that circles the grassy summit of Neutaconkanut Hill.

21 Neutaconkanut Hill

A green getaway in the thick of Providence

Distance: 1.8 miles
Time: 2 hours
Difficulty: Easy, with some rocky and steep paths

Access: From Route 10, take the Union Avenue exit and drive west to Plainfield Street. Turn right and drive to the park on the left.
Parking: Public lot at 675 Plainfield St.
Dogs: Allowed, but must be leashed
Last Date Hiked: April 2023
Trailhead GPS: 41.81168, -71.46289

PROVIDENCE—The reward for climbing to the top of Neutaconkanut Hill is to rest on a granite bench in a quiet meadow while looking out to the skyline of downtown Providence, seemingly just an arm's length away.

Sitting there, in the middle of an 88-acre park in one of the densest neighborhoods in the city, it hits home that you are surrounded by trees, trails, brooks, ledges and some of the earliest history of Providence.

The hill, inhabited for centuries by the Narragansetts, was the northwest boundary in a 1636 land agreement between sachems Canonicus and Miantonomi and Roger Williams, who founded the settlement of Providence.

The Narragansetts called the land the Great Hill of Neutaconkanut (Nu-ta-kon-ka-nut), a name with many diverse translations, including "home of squirrels," or "where the rivers flow."

Today, the city park established in 1892 is managed by the Neutaconkanut Hill Conservancy.

I parked in the public lot off Plainfield Street and for a few minutes watched youngsters do jumps in the skate park next to a playground, a pool and a recreation building.

I walked north on a paved path that skirted a ballfield and then up the hillside on a long and at times steep winding cement path to a set of steps

Neutaconkanut Hill

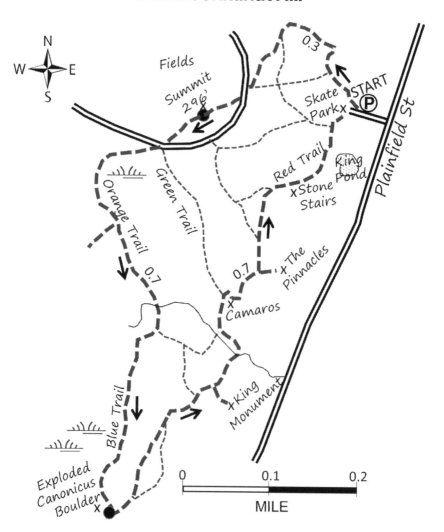

that lead to a road. I passed three birders with binoculars, a trail runner and a solo walker with a small dog.

A medallion embedded in the pavement is engraved "Built By Works Progress Administration 1935-1938." The federal program cut some of the trails and erected the trolley station at the base of the hill.

From the road, I took a path on the right by the foundation of a WPA-built bandstand where Sunday afternoon concerts in the 1930s and 1940s attracted thousands of people. The path leads to an open meadow ringed by trees.

There's also a semicircle of six granite benches. From the highest point in Providence (296 feet), you can see about 25% of the city and the tall buildings downtown.

I walked along the edge of the mowed field by Summit Ledge to a flat, orange-blazed trail that runs under oaks, hickory, birches and maples along the western perimeter of the park. After crossing a couple of boardwalks over low-lying areas, I took a short side spur west to reach the backyards of houses in Johnston before retracing my steps.

The path then crosses a wooden bridge over a rock-lined channel that seems to have been built as an aqueduct to carry water down from the top of the hill.

Just ahead, I picked up the blue-blazed trail on the right and headed up a ridge, with a hidden swamp rimmed with bright green skunk cabbage to the right, and then down to a cliff with an outcropping of sharp stones called Exploded Canonicus Boulder. One legend recounts that neighbors living below a huge glacial erratic once used as a lookout by Canonicus were worried that it would tumble down and blasted it apart to eliminate the danger.

Continuing northeast along the hillside, with Plainfield Street visible to the south, I walked to the stone King Monument, erected in 1905 as a memorial to the family of John King and Lucretia Paine King. The King family acquired the land in 1829 and built a homestead on a 16-acre portion of the hill known as King Park. Abby King, the last surviving member of the family, willed what remained of the land to the City of Providence, with the stipulation that it would not be developed.

I turned on the orange trail, crossed a stream with a channel, and then

The skyline of downtown Providence is visible from the summit of Neutaconkanut Hill, which at 296 feet, is the highest spot in the city.

found a curious site: the remains of a rusted Chevy Camaro partially buried behind a roped-off area. Thieves once stripped stolen cars there, and park managers removed at least 10 of them. But one was left as a lesson to school children studying the hill on how nature heals itself, as the car is slowly sinking in the soil.

The trail headed north to the Pinnacle Boardwalk, a walkway with a railing above a steep hillside. Just ahead, there's a vista to the right from a ledge called The Pinnacles, a series of jagged rocks that had spiritual significance to Native Americans who held ceremonies there into the 1920s. The outlook offers a view into the Silver Lake/Olneyville neighborhood below and downtown Providence in the distance.

From there, the path crosses several stone walls that once defined property lines and farmland, and then descends for several hundred yards on stone stairs to reach King Pond on the right before returning to the parking lot.

During my hike, I found some graffiti and litter, but, overall, the park is in its natural state.

I spent much of my working life in Rhode Island at The Providence Journal in downtown Providence, but I never climbed Neutaconkanut Hill. My error. It would have been a nice break from the job and would have helped me better understand the city.

22 West Warwick Greenway

A rich mill history with an unexpected sweetness

Distance: 4.5 miles
Time: 2 hours
Difficulty: Easy on flat, paved paths

Access: The bike path is accessible at several points where it intersects with side streets and roads.
Parking: Lots are available under Route 295 at the junction with West Natick Road and at Riverpoint Park. On-street parking is also available on West Warwick streets.
Dogs: Allowed, but must be leashed
Last Date Hiked: December 2022
Trailhead GPS: 41.69486, -71.53518

WEST WARWICK—The sweet scent of bath soaps is something I haven't encountered while hiking on trails across the state.

But I got a good whiff while walking across an old railroad trestle high above the South Branch of the Pawtuxet River. It came from the Bradford Soap Works, a mill complex built along the river that has been making soaps for more than 140 years.

The unexpected fragrance was a highlight of my walk along the West Warwick Greenway, a short central section of the Washington Secondary Bike Path, which stretches 19 miles through Cranston, Warwick, West Warwick, and Coventry to the Connecticut border.

Several winters ago, I started walking the Cranston leg of the bikeway after I learned that the sun quickly melts the ice and snow on the blacktopped path. In the past, I hiked the bike trail through Coventry over three mornings. After I wrote about it, a reader suggested I try the West Warwick segment to learn some history.

It was good advice.

The West Warwick Greenway runs along an old railroad bed and near several old textile mills once powered by water tumbling over man-made

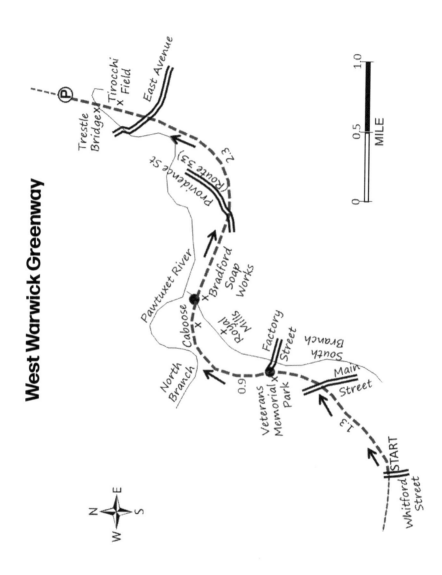

dams. The walk offers a lesson in West Warwick's industrial past and how it turned a small village into a bustling urban area.

The trail crosses the Pawtuxet River twice and passes apartments, small businesses and busy streets. One section runs through Arctic Crossing, a central intersection in town, and by several war memorials.

I set out at the border of West Warwick and Coventry where the bike path crosses Whitford Street and headed northeast on the path, which is lined in places with telephone poles and wooden posts and rail fences. I passed under a trestle that carries Route 117, one of the state's original highways, and walked along a raised part of the path by a drainage ditch. Some homeless people were living in tents below the trail.

After crossing Brookside Avenue, I walked through a cement tunnel under Main Street and emerged with a first look at the Pawtuxet River on the right. Looking through a line of trees and shrubs between the bike path and the river running below, I could see an old stone factory on the far side.

When I reached Arctic Crossing, I stopped at Veterans Memorial Park, built in 1936, and walked on a stone path to study the stone tower, two cannons and several granite monuments with plaques recognizing those lost in World War I, World War II, Korea, Beirut, and the Global War on Terror. American Legion Post 2 is adjacent to the common.

From there, I turned right on Factory Road and walked over the Sen. Francis J. LaChapelle Bridge; below were a stone dam and waterfall adjacent to the Arctic Mill. The mill's main building was built in 1865 using the stone walls of an earlier structure.

By 1885, it housed 35,824 spindles and 1,039 looms.

The mill was once a symbol of West Warwick's industrial history along the Pawtuxet River when immigrants and farmers moved to the village to work in the textile industry.

It's now closed, and current plans call for renovating it into apartments and retail space.

Returning to the bike path, I stopped to look at a kiosk with a map of the East Coast Greenway and a memorial to Adelbert "Hackey" Hackenberg (1939-2004), a volunteer who was "always ready to work and serve" on the Greenway.

The view from an old railroad trestle includes the Pawtuxet River, which tumbles over a man-made dam adjacent to the Bradford Soap Works.

There was also an arrow pointing south to "Key West 2,308 miles." I decided to save Florida for another hike.

I crossed busy Providence Street and then East Main Street, passing several rows of mill houses built for textile workers. On the horizon to the right was the clock tower and turrets of the sprawling, stone, and brick Royal Mills, which has been converted into apartments. It's an unusual sight.

Royal Mills, which began operating in the early 1800s, once manufactured Fruit of the Loom products and was the largest employer in the area. The Pawtuxet River runs between two of the largest buildings on the property.

The path passed some tennis courts on the left at Riverpoint Park, named for the junction of the north and south branches of the Pawtuxet River.

On the right, I saw a bright red New Haven Caboose, with blow-ups of Frosty the Snowman riding on one side and Santa on the other. The

The bright red New Haven Caboose is located just off the West Warwick Greenway in what was once the interchange yard of two railroads—the Hartford, Providence & Fishkill and the Pawtuxet Valley.

caboose is at what was once the interchange yard of the Hartford, Providence & Fishkill and Pawtuxet Valley railroads. Most of the rails were pulled up in the 1990s.

The Hartford, Providence, and Fishkill line, chartered in 1847, linked Providence and Hartford and later extended to the Hudson River. The railroad went bankrupt, though, and in the early 1900s, the larger New York, New Haven & Hartford railroad took over the line. The last passenger trains between Providence and Hartford ran in the 1920s, but freight service continued until 1988.

I rested and drank some water while checking out the caboose and then got back on the path. Just ahead, I crossed the high trestle where I smelled the soaps being made by Bradford Soap Works, which bills itself as the largest manufacturer of private label soaps in the world.

Two entrepreneurs from Bradford, England, started the company in the 1870s by making flake soap for use in scouring wool and then industrial lubricating soaps for New England's textile and paper industries.

After the decline of the textile industry, Bradford switched products to bar soaps that are sold worldwide through some of the biggest brand names in the business that include Aveeno, Neutrogena, Olay, Dove and Dial.

I stopped on the wide trestle and looked down at a ten-foot waterfall flowing over a dam built on the Pawtuxet River next to the old stone mill. The bike path straddles the multi-story complex, and I looked to the right at smokestacks, overhead walkways, bridges, and several other structures. Down below, a forklift moved large boxes between buildings. On the left is the more modern Broadford Soap Works factory.

Continuing on the path that bent east, I crossed Route 33 at a busy intersection called Wescott Crossing. The trail turned north into Warwick and was lined with drainage ditches and industrial buildings on one side and houses and small businesses on the other.

Entering the East Natick neighborhood, the path crossed East Avenue, where I noticed signs for a historic district, which I decided to come back to see.

I passed a solar array on the left and on the right, two workers were repairing some siding on a two-decker. Just ahead, the trail went by Tirocchi Field on the right, a trail to the river, and a sign for the East Natick Canoe Launch.

Continuing north, the path crossed an old rusted, steel truss bridge over the Pawtuxet River. Wooden plank decking and sideboards have been added for safety. It's a long way down.

I finished my walk at a dirt parking lot under Route 295 at the intersection with West Natick Road.

If you haven't been on the bike path, it's worth a walk. The Cranston section is mostly flat and straight as it runs along the backsides of small businesses and houses. The leg in Coventry is blacktop as it heads through rural, western Rhode Island and offers good looks at Johnson's Pond and the Flat River Reservoir. The trail turns to hard packed dirt as it runs closer to Connecticut.

The West Warwick link has a different, urban feel and is rich in industrial history. The sweet smells are a unique bonus.

23   Slatersville

A sidewalk journey through an historic mill village

Distance: 1.25 miles
Time: 90 minutes
Difficulty: Easy, with some small hills

Access: From Route 146, take the Slatersville/Forestdale exit and follow the Slatersville signs west to the village.
Parking: Available at lots at the post office or adjacent library
Dogs: Allowed, but must be leashed
Last Date Hiked: February 2023
Trailhead GPS: 41.99920, -71.58155

NORTH SMITHFIELD—At one point along its 10-mile course, the Branch River tumbles over a 300-foot-long dam and drops 20 feet in a crashing roar of whitewater. The wall of water sparkles in the bright sunlight on a clear, cold winter morning.

There's an equally impressive sight just downriver, where a complex network of canals, underground channels, raceways, trenches, sluice gates, bridges, dams, roads, and stone-walled buildings line the waterway.

Above that infrastructure on a hillside are tenant houses, shops, public buildings, churches and a common green.

It was all built to create Slatersville—the first planned mill village in America.

I decided to visit Slatersville after walking along the Blackstone River in downtown Pawtucket to Slater Mill, built by Samuel Slater, the father of the American Industrial Revolution. When I did some research, I learned that John Slater, Samuel's younger brother, and his wife, Ruth, set up and managed Slatersville, about 16 miles to the northwest, in the early 1800s.

After hiking through woods and farmland for most of the winter and studying the remnants of grist mills and sawmills left by early settlers, I decided to walk on some sidewalks for a change of pace and to understand a different slice of Rhode Island's history.

Slatersville

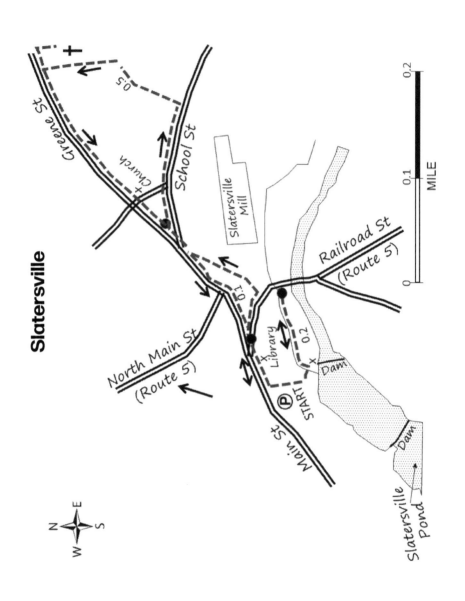

I wanted to learn more about John Slater, the lesser-known brother who arrived here from England in 1803, and the significance of what he built.

On a crisp February morning, I set out from the North Smithfield Public Library. Constructed of rubble stone, the building was once a storehouse, one of eight buildings in the Western Mill complex built by John Slater.

I walked down a short dirt path behind the library to what's now called Centennial Park on the banks of the Branch River, which forms at the confluence of the Clear and Chepachet rivers in Burrillville and flows north to Slatersville.

Looking upriver from the park, I could see the long dam with the waterfall that holds back the 170-acre Slatersville Reservoir, which supplied water to the mills.

From where I stood, the river split around me into two branches. Most of the river flowed over a curved dam, capped with granite blocks with holes where panels could be inserted to hold back water.

The other leg of the river ran into a deep, man-made, granite-block-lined canal and flowed under a 20-foot wooden bridge. Another smaller channel cut from the canal ran underground through a mechanical gate with metal and wooden gears that was designed to speed up the flow of the water to turn water wheels and create power. The elaborate engineering is a sight to see.

A footpath opened between the river and the canal, and I took it east through small trees and underbrush. To the left, on the other side of the canal, I could see an abandoned, stone, one-story building called a picker house, where raw cotton was cleaned by removing twigs, leaves, and bugs. Other buildings that formed the Western Mills are long gone.

I passed several fishing spots on the banks of the river on my right. The short path came to a ledge where the canal merged with the river before flowing over another dam and running under a stone, double-arch bridge built in 1855. The Branch River then flows through Slatersville and Forestdale before eventually emptying into the Blackstone River.

After his success at Slater Mill in Pawtucket, Samuel Slater, an immigrant who apprenticed at a mill in England, assigned his brother John to find a site for a new textile mill.

John Slater picked a spot in the dense woods where Buffum Mills, which included a sawmill, gristmill, and blacksmith's shop, was already in operation. The site offered a steep drop in the river of about 40 feet over a mile, which, once harnessed, could power textile mills.

I retraced my steps to Centennial Park, and back up to Main Street in front of the library. I then walked east with the river below me on the right until I reached Railroad Street and had my first good look at the massive Slatersville Mill.

The cotton spinning mill opened on July 4, 1807. At the time, it was the largest textile mill in America, with 1,500 spindles, and it was four times bigger than Slater Mill in Pawtucket, according to Christian de Rezendes, who produced a documentary about Slatersville.

The wooden structure burned down in 1826 and was replaced by a four-story, stone block building with a 5-story tower, reminiscent of the bell tower that once called workers to start their shifts. By 1833, the new mill, also known as Center Mill, employed 66 men, 109 women and 169 children who worked at 9,500 spindles and 225 looms to make threads and cloth, according to a report from the National Parks Service.

After the textile manufacturing industry faded in the mid-1900s, the mill building was used for several different purposes before being abandoned.

In 2007, developers renovated the structure into luxury loft apartments.

I walked through the property by following a trench that ran by the huge mill. The site also included what was once a brick weave shed built in 1824, a wooden office building, elevated walkways, bridges, and several smaller mills.

I studied the layout before taking a path up the hillside that was once used as a shortcut by workers headed from their homes down to the mills.

Unlike in the well-populated Pawtucket, where Samuel Slater built his mill, John Slater's plans required the creation of a village to attract and house workers and their families, including many from nearby farms.

When I reached the top of the hill, I got a good look at the core of the old village, which is still intact as a self-contained community of neat, well-kept houses, stores, churches, and public buildings.

I turned right on School Street and passed a common in front of a white Congregational church. The Slaters laid out the triangular green and built

Slatersville Mill in North Smithfield opened in 1807 with 1,500 spindles and was the largest textile mill in the United States.

the Greek Revival-style church, crowned with a three-stage belfry and an octagonal spire, in 1838.

Farther down School Street is the modest house where John and Ruth Slater lived and raised 11 children. They both served as resident managers and were the driving forces behind running the village.

Past the house, I took a path on the left by a gazebo with a cemetery on the right. I turned right at Greene Street, entered a gate, and on a rise in the middle of the graveyard, I found a rusted, wrought iron fence that encircled the Slater family cemetery, where John and Ruth Slater are buried.

John Slater's white marble tombstone reads:

Born at Belper, Derbyshire, England
Dec. 25, 1776
Emigrated to this country in 1803
Died May 27, 1843
Aged 66

The Branch River flows under a double-arch stone bridge before running through Slatersville and eventually emptying into the Blackstone River.

I returned to Greene Street, turned left and passed a series of historic houses and sites, including what had been a church chapel, social hall, and Union Grange Hall, which is now being used as Heritage Hall, run by the North Smithfield Heritage Association.

Down the street on the left and next to Town Hall I noticed a marker with an inscription for a dawn redwood tree: "Thought to be extinct—Discovered in China 1944."

Farther down Greene Street are a series of well-kept houses and a municipal building built in 1920 on a site that was once a hotel and boarding house.

The sidewalk slopes downhill along Main Street and by the First Commercial Block, which once housed the company store, a post office, a bank, a barbershop, a cobbler, and a hardware store. The workers used the upper floors for dances and weddings.

I finished my hike at the library, where I had started.

Following John Slater's death, his descendants ran Slatersville until

1900. Later, other owners further developed the area while renovating and preserving the core characteristics of the village.

Slatersville's success proved that mills and villages could be created outside cities, opening up the Blackstone Valley for industrialization. The model at Slatersville was replicated from Pawtucket to Worcester in places like Ashton, Albion, Lonsdale, Saylesville, and many other villages across the region.

My walk on the sidewalks in Slatersville felt different from other hikes I've taken. It helped me understand the story of the state's workers, who moved from farms to factories, and all the changes that resulted.

Geese stop traffic while crossing the road between Willow Lake and the Carousel Village at Roger Williams Park.

The iconic Temple to Music at Providence's Roger Williams Park can be seen across Cunliff Lake from the white diamond trail.

24   Roger Williams Park

Rhode Island's urban jewel

Distance: 3.5 miles
Time: 2 hours
Difficulty: Easy

Access: Entrances to the park are located on Park Avenue in Cranston and on Elmwood Avenue and Broad Street in Providence.
Parking: Available in several lots
Dogs: Allowed, but must be leashed
Last Date Hiked: April 2023
Trailhead GPS: 41.77712, -71.41431

PROVIDENCE—Gaggles of geese have the right of way in Roger Williams Park, crossing roads and blocking traffic until a park worker drives up in a jeep with yellow lights flashing and horn honking to coax them out of harm's way. This scene reminded me of Robert McCloskey's classic children's book *Make Way for Ducklings.*

And here in one of Rhode Island's marquee parks, geese, ducks, swans, chipmunks, and squirrels intermingle with statues, memorials and monuments on tree-lined paths that edge seven ponds in the urban retreat.

It's a great place to take a relaxing walk and learn some history.

In 1871, Betsey Williams, the great-great-great-granddaughter of Roger Williams, the founder of Rhode Island, donated 102 acres of farmland in her will to create the park. More woods and ponds were purchased in 1892 for $359,000 to expand the park to 427 acres, including 90 acres of water.

When I visited recently, I hoped to circle many of the ponds on a flat, easy trail while I recovered from a minor hiking injury. A 3.2-mile loop, called the Big Lakes Trail, gave me what I wanted.

I set out from the kayak launch off Frederick C. Green Memorial Boulevard and walked north on the white diamond trail along the banks of Cunliff Lake.

Native trees and grasses planted along a short causeway between Cunliff

Roger Williams Park

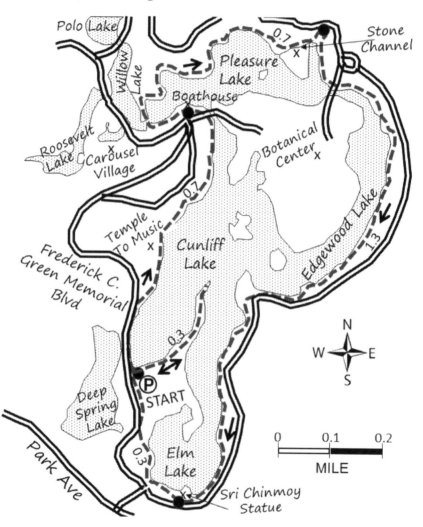

Lake and Deep Spring Lake create what's called a bioswale garden, which filters contaminants from storm runoff before it enters the water.

The path continues along the shore and runs behind the Temple to Music, designed in 1924 by William T. Aldrich and built of white Vermont marble. The opening, commemorated with a performance by the U.S. Marine Band, attracted 50,000 to the natural amphitheater, ringed with giant oak trees, on the slope just above the temple.

After another hundred yards, I climbed a small hill and passed The Pancratiast, a statue of a weary fighter that is a copy of a Roman sculpture discovered in 1885 near the ancient Baths of Constantine. I crossed Cladrastis Avenue and walked west by the Clark Dalrymple Boathouse, named for the philanthropist who funded the construction. The Queen Anne-style structure is now the headquarters of the park, owned by the City of Providence.

I walked down a sidewalk and noticed the Carousel Village on the left, where I saw geese clogging the road. I turned right and crossed a black iron bridge connecting Pleasure Lake, where swan boats cruise, and Willow Lake. Only two willows are still standing.

After the bridge, the dirt path winds along the lake and through some thickets where I startled some ducks. Just ahead, a sidewalk with a weathered "WPA" shield embedded in the concrete leads up a hillside.

The Works Progress Administration, created by President Franklin Roosevelt to put people to work during the Depression, built many of the park's sidewalks, roads, and bridges. The sidewalk leads up to the yellow-brick Museum of Natural History across the road from The Fighting Gladiator, a bronze recast of a Roman marble original displayed in the Louvre in Paris.

Just to the north is a 12-foot bronze statue of Abraham Lincoln standing tall on a 10-ton granite base.

I retraced my steps to the white diamond trail around Pleasure Lake and passed a fisherman who was reeling in a 13-pound carp. He said they can run up to 30 pounds, and he'll fish until the water freezes over.

The path then narrows through a muddy area and along a channel that directs water off the hillside and away from the Edgewood neighborhood. I spotted Flower Island offshore and fountains spraying water. Several swans swam in a quiet cove.

The path crossed Cladrastis Avenue, which runs south by the Mounted Patrol. I stayed straight on the white diamond trail that shrank to a footpath through shrubs and woods and offered views across Edgewood Lake to the rear of the Botanical Center.

The trail followed the shore and turned south for about a half mile, passing under sweetgums and spruce trees before reaching the southern tip of Elm Lake. A dozen geese waddled by a bronze statue of Sri Chinmoy, an Indian spiritual leader, poet, artist, and composer who founded the World Harmony Run.

A few steps away, the lake spills down a 10-step waterfall into a stream that flows under an arched stone bridge and eventually to Narragansett Bay.

I sat on a bench under paper birch and maple trees and watched the geese before picking up the path that continued behind a baseball field and to a side trail. That path runs along a short peninsula, offering another view of the Temple to Music across Cunliff Lake before returning to the kayak launch where I started.

If you don't want to follow the dirt path, you can circle the ponds on the paved walkways or the bike lanes along most of the roads. You'll still be able to see most of the statues and the other features. Signs in English and Spanish will guide your walk and others advise not to feed the waterfowl.

Before you leave, head toward the park's Elmwood Avenue entrance to see the cottage once occupied by Betsey Williams, whose will required the creation of a monument to Roger Williams. His 27-foot-tall monument, erected in 1877 next to the cottage, was the first statue built in the park. And rightly so.

Coastal Hikes

The crescent-shaped rocky shoreline curls along the perimeter trail as it hugs the scenic coast at Sachuest Point National Wildlife Refuge in Middletown.

25 Sachuest Point National Wildlife Refuge

A birder's paradise along Rhode Island Sound

Distance: 2.8 miles
Time: 1.75 hours
Difficulty: Easy, wide, flat trails

Access: From the north, follow Route 138 to Route 138A. Take a left on Prospect Avenue and a right on Paradise Avenue to Sachuest Point Road to the preserve. From the south, follow Route 138 and take Miantonomi Avenue and Green End Avenue. Turn south on Paradise Avenue and then take a left on Sachuest Point Road.
Parking: Available at a large lot at the Visitor Center
Dogs: Not allowed
Last Date Hiked: August 2021
Trailhead GPS: 41.48113, -71.24429

MIDDLETOWN—My brother, Peter, visited from Florida and wanted to see Rhode Island's coastline and what makes the state special. I took him to Sachuest Point, and he wasn't disappointed.

Peter enjoyed the views and the booms of the waves crashing on the rocks, the fragrant and colorful wildflowers that lined the wide, easy-to-walk paths and the birds and their tweets from the underbrush along the trail.

He spotted an American goldfinch and paused to study its vibrant yellow coloring.

Sachuest Point is a 422-acre wildlife refuge and stopover for more than 200 species of migratory birds. The free public preserve is popular with walkers of all skill levels and annually attracts 65,000 visitors who try to catch a look at birds and wildlife in a beautiful setting while also learning some history.

From the mid-1600s to the early 1900s, farmers grazed sheep and raised crops on the peninsula. During World War I, two 4.7-inch Armstrong

Sachuest Point National Wildlife Refuge

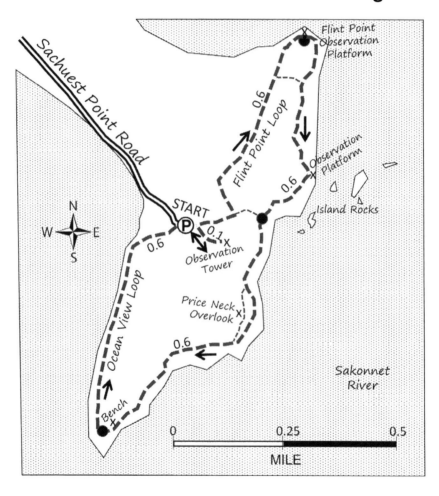

guns were sent from Boston Harbor to Sachuest to protect the coast from German U-boats.

During World War II, the U.S. Navy used the property as a rifle range and as a key post in a communications network along the coast to monitor enemy ships on Narragansett Bay.

In 1970, the Audubon Society donated 70 acres that began the process of combining adjoining parcels to create Sachuest Point National Wildlife Refuge.

Our walk started at the Visitor Center, and we took a short gravel path to an observation tower in the interior of the refuge to get a good overview of the preserve. Then, we retraced our steps and set out on a perimeter trail, called the Flint Point Loop, that crossed several fields before entering a dense section of shrubs and vines.

After about a quarter mile, we reached the Flint Point observation platform, just a few steps high, where saltwater surf fishermen cast lines from the rocks below. To the northwest, across a salt marsh, we saw Third Harbor, filled with boats, and Third Beach, where only a few swimmers were in the water on an overcast morning.

The path, lined with rosa rugosa hedges, turned south, and we noted the first of eight marked side spurs that lead down to the rocks and shoreline.

After about a quarter mile, we stopped at a low observation deck alongside the trail with mounted telescopes to look across the Sakonnet River to Little Compton. In the foreground, a landmark called Island Rocks emerged from the sea, covered with dozens of sea birds. Below us on the shore, a father and two children with a bucket searched for sea life in the pools among the rocks.

There's a cutoff on the right that lets walkers shorten their hike and leads back to the Visitor Center. We stayed on the perimeter trail and noted that with the ocean on our left and dense shrubs, vines, native grasses and small trees on the right, the interior of the sanctuary creates a safe habitat for raptors, migratory ducks, birds and wildlife.

Just ahead, we climbed a side trail, called Price Neck Overlook Trail, to a series of ledges. We had learned at a kiosk at the trailhead that the stony ledges were once part of Africa, left behind when the supercontinent of Pangaea split apart 200 million years ago.

Several cormorants dry their wings while perched on exposed offshore rocks on the western side of Sachuest Point.

The path descended from the ledges to Sachuest Point, a series of huge boulders and outcroppings at the southern tip of the preserve that juts into Rhode Island Sound. We paused, sat on a bench, and enjoyed the panoramic view of the ocean on three sides. There we spotted Sakonnet Lighthouse across the water and watched several sailboats and fishing trawlers cruise the bay.

The trail turned north, with a view west over the channel to Newport and the top of the Pell Bridge. We stopped for a look at several seagulls and dark-colored cormorants that perched on some offshore rocks and spread their wings to dry.

The path returned to the Visitor Center while offering views across Sachuest Bay, to Second Beach and the causeway that leads to the refuge. Far in the distance, the stately spires of St. George's School can be seen on a grassy hillside.

During our walk on the wide, well-maintained trail, we exchanged greetings with walkers, trail runners, fishermen, tourists speaking foreign languages, and families, one with a child in a stroller.

Some stopped at the end of the walk to read two message boards. On one, children had scrawled the names of the wildlife and birds they had spotted: mice, rabbits, deer, ants, monarch butterflies, bees, shrimp, yellow warblers, white cranes and laughing seagulls.

The other cautioned that since 1970, 2.9 billion birds had disappeared, largely because of loss of habitat and commercial development.

Hopefully, we'll still see American goldfinches the next time we visit.

Side spurs lead down the cliffs above the West Passage to hidden, rocky beaches.

26 Beavertail State Park

At every step, stunning coastal vistas and historical surprises

Distance: 3.5 miles
Time: 2.5 hours
Difficulty: Easy to moderate on the rocky shoreline

Access: Off Route 138 east, take the first exit after the Jamestown Verrazzano Bridge. Drive six miles through the center of Jamestown and by Mackerel Cove to the park entrance.
Parking: Available, at public lots
Dogs: Allowed, but must be leashed
Last Date Hiked: June, 2021
Trailhead GPS: 41.45152, -71.39742

JAMESTOWN—Beavertail Lighthouse, a beacon that has guided ships through shoals and reefs at the entrance of Narragansett Bay since 1749, is the best-known landmark on the southern tip of Conanicut Island.

The announcement that the U.S. Coast Guard is giving up ownership of the third-oldest lighthouse in the country has only increased its profile. I observed the 64-foot tower during a recent hike in Beavertail State Park, but I also wanted to see the lesser-known, hidden natural features on the peninsula and what's left of its top-secret military history. I found some of both.

I set out from Parking Lot 3. The view on a crystal-clear morning was stunning down the rocky coast and across the East Passage, with Brenton Point visible about two miles away. Sailboats of all sizes, power boats, tankers, ferries and fishing boats cruised the Bay.

Just down the banks from the lot are the Payton Blocks. The huge, carved granite stones were lost at sea during a snowstorm in 1859 when the schooner Harvey F. Payton, which was carrying the blocks from Boston to a government building site in Alexandria, Virginia, was shipwrecked. The Hurricane of 1938 flung the stones onto the shore.

I walked north on the grassy banks and found the earth-covered Battery Whiting munitions bunker. Part of Fort Burnside built in 1942, it served

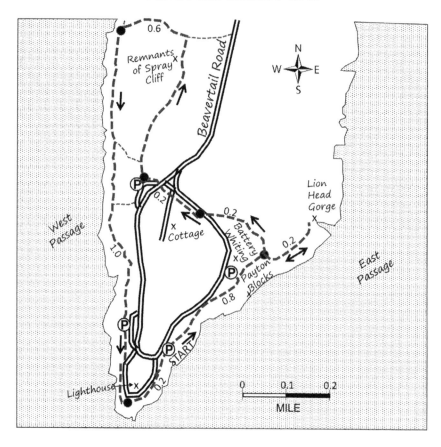

The Beavertail Lighthouse and surrounding buildings, as viewed from the rocks along the East Passage, stand on the southern tip of Conanicut Island.

as a key post in the picket-line defense of the coast during World War II. The circular gun turrets for the cannons that guarded the Bay and were manned by the R.I. National Guard are still there.

At low tide, I walked down the banks and northeast on the white-streaked, dark rocks. In about a quarter mile, I reached Lion Head Gorge, named for the crash of the waves into the cleft that sounds like a lion's roar. My arrival scattered dozens of seagulls perched on the 30-foot cliffs that line the chasm.

I could have stayed all day watching the white plumes of salt spray, the lighthouse back over my shoulder, Castle Hill across the passage and the Pell Bridge to the northeast. But there were still miles to go.

Retracing my steps, I climbed a side path up the banks and picked up the Green Dot trail, which runs through a thicket of small trees and brush. I found an abandoned Quonset-style hut and several cement anchors with eyelets that may have held cables to support 12 antennas, a transmitter and radio equipment. The tallest antenna, at 624 feet, was named 1-Juliet.

The historic Beavertail Lighthouse has guided ships through the entrance of Narragansett Bay since 1749.

The U.S. Navy built the station in the 1960s with new technology to communicate covertly with submarines underwater and with a network that included Sachuest Point and Newport. Two months after the antenna was installed, a small plane flying from Washington, D.C., hit a guy wire and crashed, killing the pilot and two passengers. The system was later taken down.

I continued west, crossed a road, and saw to the left a communications tower and two observation platforms that surrounded a brown-shingled house. During World War II, the building served as the Harbor Entrance Command Post, which monitored submarine nets, minefields and listening posts in the passages.

Disguised as a farmhouse, the bomb proof building had walls 3 feet thick and a bunker underneath. The road to the property is now marked "Authorized Vehicles Only" and the building is leased to a tenant, according to the park's owner, the Rhode Island Department of Environmental Management.

Crossing the park's entrance road, I took the red dot trail north through white, fragrant wildflowers. Songbirds chirped in the hemlock groves. We walked over paved paths that were part of SprayCliff, a secret research, development and testing site. U.S. Navy and MIT engineers worked there to design night radar that U.S. planes used to intercept Japanese aircraft.

The unblazed trail looped west and along cliffs above the West Passage, with views north to Quonset, west to Narragansett and south to Point Judith, 7.2 miles away. I followed the cliffs, passing side spurs down rocky ledges to tiny beaches. The steepness and loose rock on the paths looked dangerous.

After about a mile, I headed down to the rocks through rosa rugosa hedges with white and pink flowers and walked south by tidal pools and rock formations. I reached the point, a beautiful but treacherous spot just below the lighthouse. During storms, scuba divers, fishermen, tourists and thrill seekers have been injured. Some have drowned.

Among the rocks is the octagonal base of the wooden lighthouse built in 1749. It burned down and was replaced by a rubble tower until 1856, when the current granite lighthouse was built. The Coast Guard plans to continue to operate the automated beacon, but the National Park Service has recommended that ownership of the lighthouse be transfered to the

Lion Head Gorge, on the northeast corner of Beavertail State Park, is named for the crashing waves that sound like a lion's roar.

DEM, which manages the surrounding property in collaboration with the Beavertail Lighthouse Museum Association.

Surrounding the lighthouse are markers for several offshore features, including the base of Whale Rock Light, which was destroyed by the Hurricane of 1938 and looks like a submarine turret, and the location where U.S. warships sank the German U-boat 853 in 1945.

I returned to Lot 3 where I started. But before leaving, I drove the loop through the 153-acre park, finding another bunker and gun turret left from Battery 213.

By late morning, sunbathers, readers, picnickers, photographers and sightseers filled the rocks and grasslands on the peninsula, which is shaped like the tail of a beaver.

It's quite a place, a unique mixture of stunning natural beauty, striking rock formations on the coastline and a secret military history.

27   Napatree Point

Where sea views, birdwatching and military history converge

Distance: 3.3 miles
Time: 2 hours
Difficulty: Easy, mostly beach walking

Access: Take 1A south to Watch Hill Road through Avondale Drive south into Watch Hill to Fort Road.
Parking: Limited on-street parking and in a small nearby lot
Dogs: Allowed on leashes but restricted to 6 p.m. to 8 a.m. from May 2 until Labor Day
Last Date Hiked: May 2021
Trailhead: 41.31004, -71.85866

WESTERLY—Napatree Point, a J-shaped finger of land that curls for a mile and a half into the ocean, has been changing its profile, over and over, for centuries.

When Dutch trader Adriaen Block explored the coast in 1614, he spied the heavily wooded peninsula and named it for the nap, or nape, of trees.

In 1815, the Great September Gale blew down all the trees, leaving a barren barrier spit of land.

By the 1930s, the sandy strip was dotted with cottages, but the Hurricane of 1938 washed them away, killing 15 people.

Storms and rising seas have continued to alter the landform, moving the slim strip north by several hundred feet during the last 80 years and reshaping the "J" hook.

What hasn't changed, however, is the unspoiled natural beauty of the pristine beaches, the view for miles in all directions, the seabirds, and the easy walk to the most southern and western end of mainland Rhode Island.

I set out on a spring morning from the Watch Hill village and strolled west through the quiet business district, with the Watch Hill Yacht Club on the right and a string of private cabanas on the left. Tourists, boaters, and swimmers had not yet arrived for the summer.

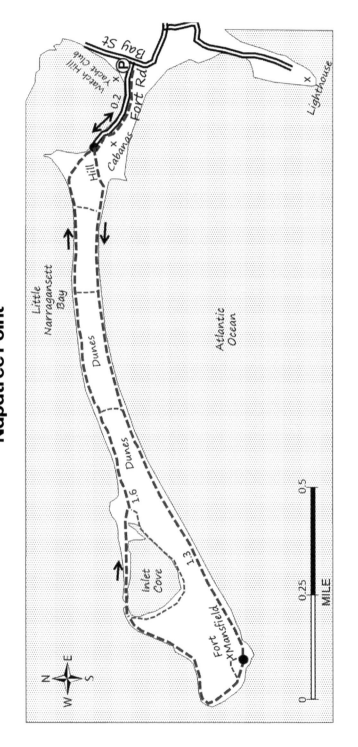

The pristine, sickle-shaped beach on the southern side of Napatree Point extends west for about 1.5 miles.

At the end of a chain-link fence at the trailhead, there's a sign marking the entrance to the public conservation area, managed by the Watch Hill Conservancy and Fire District.

After a short walk in the soft sand, the trail splits.

I went left to the top of a small hill to see a long, narrow stretch of beach to the west. Over my left shoulder and to the south stood a breakwater and the Watch Hill Lighthouse.

I walked on the firm sand at the shoreline, just down the beach from the strip of shells and small stones smoothed by the rolling surf. As the ocean lapped the shore, small shorebirds played tag with the waves.

Further up the beach, the deep, soft, white sand is tiring to trudge through. There's also a lengthy dune at the top of the rise that is covered with plants, bushes, and grass. It's roped off to protect the nests and eggs of endangered birds, including piping plovers and least terns.

I passed an osprey pole but saw no signs of the large, fish-eating hawks.

After a mile or so, there's a strange, T-shaped tower in the brambles on the dune. A sign explained that it's a solar-powered radio antenna that tracks bats and migratory birds, part of a series of stations along the Atlantic Seaboard.

Just ahead is the tip of the point of land, with vertical pilings and huge black stones.

I found a narrow side trail on the right that wandered through thickets and up a slope to the ruins of Fort Mansfield, now fenced off and covered with graffiti. The bunkers and gun turrets are still visible.

The federal government opened the fort in 1901 to defend the entrance to Long Island Sound and New York City. But a mock battle in 1907 exposed a design flaw where invading ships could bombard the fort, but the installation's artillery couldn't reach the intruders. The fort was abandoned in 1909.

A spur from the fort leads down to a quarter-mile half circle of shoreline around the western rim of the point. The beach is filled with boulders of all sizes.

I rested on a large, warm, smooth stone, smelled the salt air and listened to the squawks of seagulls, the boom of waves striking the shore, the clang of bells in the buoys marking the channel, and the blast of a horn from a passing ferry.

Looking out, I spotted Sandy Point, an island in Little Narragansett Bay that was once part of a 1½-mile-long, sickle-shaped northern extension of Napatree Point. But the Hurricane of 1938 cut several breaches in the spit and separated what is now Sandy Island from the land.

Napatree Point is a moraine, formed by the accumulation of sand and rock deposited by moving glaciers during the Ice Age. Watching the crash of the waves, I could easily understand how the land is changing because of a geologic process called longshore drift. Wind, waves, and tides push sand onto Napatree and build dunes. Storms erode the sand and return it to the ocean and bay, constantly reshaping the peninsula.

After climbing to a 20-foot cliff above the rocky beach, I followed a path north and down again to the beach, littered with timbers, broken lobster traps, pieces of concrete and seaweed.

I followed the shore to the hook of the "J." It was low tide, and a narrow channel of water drained from the inland cove to the sea.

I took off my boots, crossed the shallow water and sat on the other

Watch Hill Lighthouse has been a nautical beacon for ships since 1754.

Visitors to Napatree Point can rest on large smooth stones off the western shore and watch ferries, fishing boats and other vessels cruise Little Narragansett Bay.

side to dry off. (Beware: Hikers should check the tides to make sure they are able to cross.)

To the northwest is the Connecticut coast and Stonington. I also studied the opening of the Pawcatuck River and then scanned northeast to the waterfront mansions. (Taylor Swift's property is on the other side of Watch Hill.)

Continuing east on the beach, I passed another inland osprey pole, a photographer and a couple of sunbathers. The protected harbor is dotted with dozens of bobbing white moorings identified by the names or numbers of owners.

I followed the edge of the water along the soft, white sandy beach and finished where I started.

After living in Rhode Island for decades, I realized this was the first time I had explored the southernmost and westernmost point of the mainland. It will not be the last.

28 Black Point

A spectacular, rugged coastline leading to stone-walled ruins

Distance: 1.8 miles
Time: 1.5 hours
Difficulty: Easy, with some rocky trails

Access: From Scarborough State Beach, drive 1.5 miles north to a small lot on the right
Parking: Available for about 20 cars
Dogs: Allowed, but must be leashed
Last Date Hiked: November 2022
Trailhead GPS: 41.40011, -71.46471

NARRAGANSETT—Every time I visited Scarborough State Beach during the summer, I would look north along the shore and wonder about the stone-walled ruins at the edge of the rocky coastline.

I knew they were just south of Black Point, the focus of a 5-year fight between developers and environmentalists in the 1980s, but other than that, they were a mystery to me.

So, after the sunbathers and beach walkers disappeared, I decided to explore the area with my brother Peter, who was visiting from Florida and wanted to see and learn about Rhode Island's coast. And we discovered some history along the way.

On an early fall day, we set out from a pullout lot and headed east on a wide trail. In a short distance, the main trail went straight, but we went left on a smaller, grassy footpath that wound through thick shrubland. The noise from cars on Ocean Road and the occasional chiming bells from the Christian Brothers Center across the road soon faded and were replaced by the sounds of birds tweeting in the bushes and waves crashing against rocks.

The path passed under a canopy of trees before bending toward the sea and then along a cliff above the ocean. We stopped for a good, long sweeping look that included lobster traps bobbing offshore and a half-dozen fishing boats motoring across Narragansett Bay.

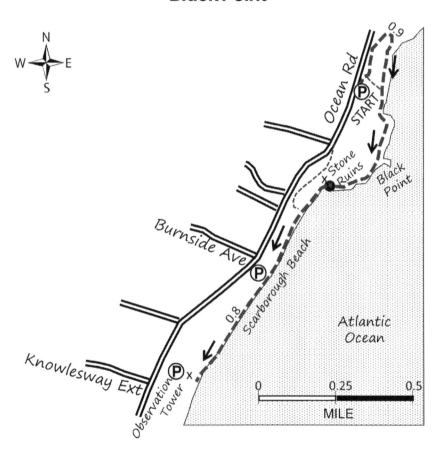

Just ahead was a four-way intersection. On the right was the path back to the parking lot and to the left was a trail down a slope to the ocean. We saved the path straight ahead for later.

We took the left option down, crossing ledges and giant boulders. Some were bleached yellow and light orange from the sun and saltwater while the rocks at the shoreline and underwater at high tide were black. We found a rusted fence bolted into the rocks but had no clue about who put it there.

Fishermen were spaced out about 20 yards apart on the rocks, casting long fishing poles and trying to hook sea bass.

To the north along the coast, there were several mansions perched off Bass Rock and above a rock-lined cove. To the south, the shoreline jutted into the ocean to form what's called Black Point.

Some say the name, Black Point, is derived from the color of the rocks that stretch into the sea. Others say the site was named for the SS Black Point, a coal ship that was sunk in 1945 by a German U-boat just off the shore. It was the last ship sunk in World War II.

The more recent history of the area includes a developer's plans in the 1980s to build 80 condominiums at Black Point on what was one of the last long stretches of undeveloped shoreline along the West Bay. Environmentalists, however, argued that the 42-acre site had been used for outdoor recreation for generations, and footpaths gave the public access to the shoreline.

For five years, there were public protests against the project, and the developer and environmentalists fought in court and before regulatory bodies.

In 1989, the state decided to condemn the land, take the property, offer the developer $6.4 million and preserve Black Point as a state-managed public preserve. One of the trails to the coast is dedicated to Malcolm Grant, a Rhode Island Department of Environmental Management official who worked to acquire Black Point.

After surveying the shoreline, my brother and I walked back up the cliff and took the path south. Several side spurs lead down to barnacle-encrusted rocks, tidal pools and outcroppings smoothed by the waves and covered with sea birds.

One spur passed a hand-lettered wooden cross inscribed with the word "Alou"—a truncated way of saying, "I love you"—and dedicated to Erica

The remains of a carriage house with stone walls stand on the coastline between Black Point and Scarborough State Beach in Narragansett.

Lee Knowles, who was killed in a drunken-driving car crash in 2012. After the sign was put up, it disappeared and was later found floating off the coast of eastern Long Island. A resident there returned it to Rhode Island.

While we studied the sign, a fisherman and his buddy passed us, and I asked if it was a good morning to catch sea bass.

"If we're lucky," one replied.

We continued on the path as it wound along the shore until I could see Scarborough State Beach as it stretched along the shoreline. Point Judith Lighthouse was far in the distance to the south.

Below us were a broken seawall and a storm fence on the cliff. I thought we might have missed the ruins we were searching for until they appeared just above the bushes off the path to the right.

We explored a bit and found two end walls about 25 feet tall, built of round stones that were covered with a yellow growth. Stone steps led inside, where small trees and shrubs grew. The roof and windows were long gone. Graffiti was spray-painted on the inside walls.

A fisherman casts for sea bass off the rocks just north of Black Point.

A walker we passed told us the ruins once formed a carriage house that was part of a huge estate, called Windswept. Later, our research found that a mansion, perched between Black Point and Scarborough Beach, was built by the Davis family—one of many erected by wealthy Rhode Islanders along the coastline at the turn of the 20th century.

Perry Davis, the family patriarch, made a fortune in the 1850s by creating an elixir, called Perry Davis' Vegetable Pain Killer, made with myrrh, camphor alcohol and opium. The remedy promised to cure cholera, colic, dysentery, and other common afflictions and is considered to have been the first nationally advertised drug for chronic pain.

Perry's grandson, Edmund Perry, later sold the painkiller and used the proceeds to build Windswept in 1895. The 21-room mansion had five bedrooms, a kitchen, laundry, pantry, living areas and servants' quarters.

In the 1900s, the property was sold to a pair of brothers who renovated the mansion into a high-end restaurant, called Cobb's by the Sea.

In 1952, the Albert Lownes family acquired the property but never occupied it. The vacant mansion was plagued by vandals, fires and storms and was later demolished. In the 1970s, the state DEM purchased the land.

We found several paved walkways and roads behind the carriage house, telephone poles and two 5-foot stone pillars that may have once marked the entrance to the property.

Any other remains were camouflaged by a thick tangle of shrubs, bushes, and other vegetation, so we headed back to the beach and crossed a broken sea wall and some large, rectangular cement slabs.

We headed south across the sand that in summer is covered with sunbathers. Now, just a few walkers walked the public beach, bundled up against the wind.

Continuing on, we passed a cement retaining wall on the right and then a boardwalk, pavilion, concession stand and gazebo. All were boarded up.

We finished our hike just before Scarborough South at a roofed observation tower. We climbed the structure and looked north to see the ruins. A hundred years ago, the mansion must have been quite a sight. We also tried to envision what Black Point would have looked like if condos covered the shoreline.

In its natural state, the rocky coastline is spectacular.

29 Goddard Memorial State Park

A hike into a little-known piece of Rhode Island aviation history

Distance: 4.5 miles
Time: 2.5 hours
Difficulty: Easy, on flat paved roads and dirt paths

Access: Off Route 1, take Old Forge Road to Ives Road. Park entrances are on the left.
Parking: Available, in a large lot
Dogs: Allowed
Last Date Hiked: March 2021
Trailhead GPS: 41.66683, -71.43252

WARWICK—Rhode Island is full of surprising, one-of-a-kind places with rich histories that you sometimes discover on the way to someplace else.

I stumbled on one while driving on Post Road to Goddard Memorial State Park (more on that hike later.)

I stopped at a sign for "Chepiwanoxet," and read that Native Americans fished from a nearby island before Colonial farmers divided the land into "thatch lots" and harvested salt marsh hay for livestock feed. Later, after a railroad station opened in the 1830s, a hotel, shore dinner hall and small cottages formed a beach resort.

The sign also reported that the island was the site of the first airplane factory in the United States. The seaplanes tested and built there were flown in World War I.

I decided to see the site for myself and drove a short distance to Chepiwanoxet Point, where another sign explained that Edson Gallaudet, a Yale physics professor, built a plant there with the backing of Rhode Island investors. He designed and manufactured an amphibious aircraft that set world records for rate of climb and speed. The planes were purchased by the Navy and Army for use in the war. Later, Gallaudet's company changed hands several times and eventually merged with Electric Boat to form General Dynamics Corp.

Goddard State Memorial Park

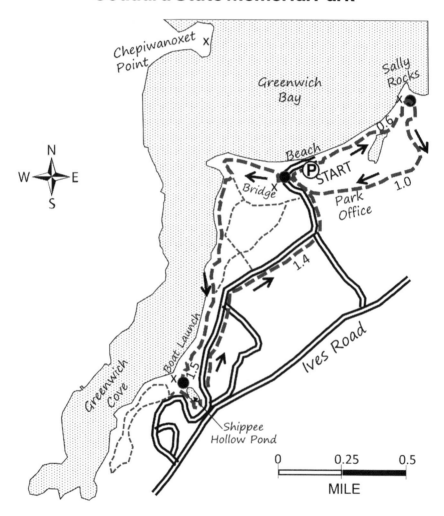

I explored the island, now a city park, on a 0.4-mile perimeter path and found a fire pit and two benches looking out on Greenwich Bay. The Warwick Conservation Commission has put up markers on trees, identifying 18 types.

If you look closely, you can see cement foundations, pilings, bricks from an old kiln, broken timbers, the remains of bulkheads and huge chunks of concrete from structures wrecked by hurricanes that battered the island.

With thoughts of military seaplanes buzzing over Greenwich Bay, I continued to Goddard, parked at the beach, and walked northeast and slightly uphill to a wide path on a bank about 20 feet above the water. There were many side cuts to the shore below and great views through the trees to the houses on the other side of the bay. I passed a frozen-over pond on the right and heard water rushing through two culverts under the path. I kept bearing to the left as other paths crossed the trail until I saw some houses just ahead. A side path led me down to the beach to Sally Rocks, a string of black boulders stretching into the sea.

From there, I looked west across the bay to Chepiwanoxet and could make out the causeway that Gallaudet built in 1916 to connect the mainland to the island. I learned later that a test pilot, Jack McGee, became the first aircraft casualty in Rhode Island when a pontoon on the Gallaudet seaplane he was flying dipped and struck a swell. The plane flipped and McGee drowned just off the point where I was standing.

I retraced my steps and took a different, little-used path along the east side of the pond before bushwhacking to a road that led by the nine-hole golf course on the left and then to the park office. I talked with an employee who said nobody knew where the name Sally Rocks came from. But when I mentioned Chepiwanoxet, his eyes lit up. He knew of the old seaplane factory and said that he'd once found staples on the rocky beaches after metal waste was dumped on the island.

I returned to the trail and walked by a boarded-up carousel building and a stone marker for a time capsule that was buried in 2009 and set to be opened in 2109. I crossed a pedestrian bridge over a road and headed back into the woods via a trail on a bank above the bay. After a half mile or so, a side trail led to Long Point, and I had a closer look at Chepiwanoxet, a Narragansett word that means "little separated place." The peninsula and triangular island looked like a prime site for launching seaplanes.

A string of black boulders, called Sally Rocks, stretches from the beach into Greenwich Bay from the northeast corner of Goddard Memorial State Park in Warwick.

A pedestrian bridge at Goddard Memorial State Park in Warwick passes over a roadway and leads to a path on the banks of Greenwich Bay.

I returned to the main trail, sometimes frozen and slippery, and could see a marina across the cove. It was another mile or so to a boat launch. About 50 yards south is Shippee Hollow Pond, which was frozen and sometimes is used for skating. I rested there for a few minutes before walking up to the road that runs through the park and returning to the parking lot.

There are 18 miles of mostly unmarked trails, bridle paths and walkways in the 490-acre state park. Many people were walking on the network of roads around fields and picnic sites.

The grounds were once the estate of Robert Goddard, a Civil War officer and Rhode Island politician. There's a weathered plaque on a stone pillar at the park's entrance noting that his children donated the land to the state in 1927.

All that's interesting, but not as much as leaving a busy main road to find an isolated island where an entrepreneur in the 1910s designed, built, and launched seaplanes that helped win a world war.

That's a unique Rhode Island story.

30 Ninigret National Wildlife Refuge

An ocean coastal walk with a surprise visit to the Navy's "Charlietown"

Distance: 5.3 miles
Time: 2.5 hours
Difficulty: Easy, flat wide paths

Access: Off Route 1, look for the signs for Ninigret Park and turn southeast.
Parking: Available at the entrance to Ninigret Park or farther down a road in a lot at the Ninigret National Wildlife Refuge
Dogs: Not allowed
Last Date Hiked: May 2022
Trailhead GPS: 41.372123, -71.664194

CHARLESTOWN—The Grassy Point Trail winds across a peninsula covered with small trees, shrubs, and native grasses to an outlook above Ninigret Pond, the largest coastal salt pond in Rhode Island.

The Narragansett Tribe once fished here, built villages along the shoreline, and hunted in the oak and maple forests. Now, flat-bottomed boats cruise the pond to harvest traps filled with oysters and mussels.

Inland from the pond, there are salt marshes, mudflats, kettle ponds, freshwater wetlands, and maritime shrublands in the Ninigret National Wildlife Refuge. The sanctuary attracts 250 species of birds, especially during the migratory season, and 70 nest here.

Two friends and I set out to explore Ninigret Pond and the 409-acre nature preserve. We started out from a massive, asphalt-covered lot, quite a contrast to the natural area we would soon visit, at the entrance to Ninigret Park, owned by the Town of Charlestown. We parked by a granite Navy memorial inscribed with the words, "Through these portals pass the hottest pilots in the world."

From 1943-1973, the site served as the Charlestown Naval Auxiliary Landing Field, called "Charlietown" by the young night fighter pilots. Many of the 1,500 men stationed there were trained to fly, including George H.W. Bush, who later became the 41st president. In its heyday, the base had 150

An angler wades into Ninigret Pond to fly cast for stripers.

buildings, including hangars, mess halls, bunkers, barracks, administration offices, radio transmitters, a wastewater treatment plant, and a fire station. Most are long gone, but you can still see the remains of the three runways (each 200 feet wide and 4,800 feet long), two taxiways and rings in the asphalt that were used to tie down the 300 planes, including Hellcats and Avengers, that were parked there.

We walked across the lot, used now for parking for the annual Charlestown Seafood Festival, and noted the town's playgrounds and ballfields on the left. We picked up a bike path that paralleled a road and followed it by the gray-domed Frosty Drew Observatory, which opens on Fridays for stargazers.

Across the paved road is a nature center, under a sprawling willow tree next to Little Nini Pond and a sandy beach. Red and yellow bobbers caught in branches on the banks indicate the pond's a fishing spot, too.

We continued down the road, noticed red blazes on the right and took a short loop trail through dense vegetation before reemerging onto the road.

Ahead is the entrance to the Ninigret National Wildlife Refuge, with a parking lot, bathroom, and kiosk with a map of the area.

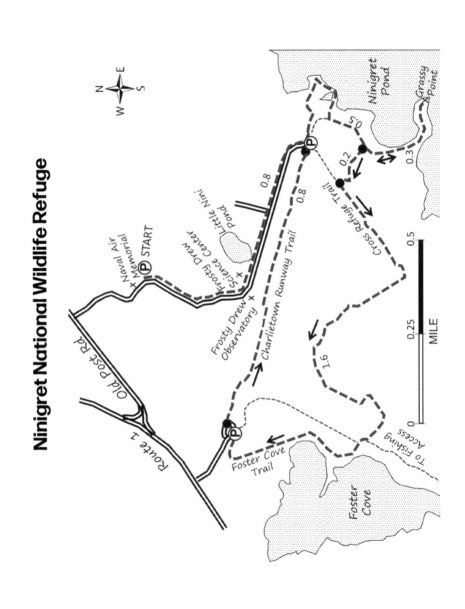

We went left on a dirt path and got our first whiff of the ocean from a sea breeze coming from the east before reaching another asphalt lot. This one is painted with a white "30" in huge block numbers to mark Runway 30, named for the first two digits of the compass reading used by pilots to find the spot. We also passed remnants of landing lights, poles, and foundations.

At this point, the path loops through a habitat restoration area to the northern edge of Ninigret Pond, which is bracketed with private property on the left.

Across the pond is a line of cottages along a barrier beach. A fishing boat crossed the water. Several cormorants stood offshore on some rocks while an egret walked across some mud flats and an osprey soared overhead.

The trail skirts a small pond and crosses a wooden bridge next to a kayak and canoe launch. We picked up the Grassy Point Trail and headed south along the edge of Ninigret Pond before turning east on the peninsula. The wide path of crushed stone eventually passed a bench before ending at a rise in the land with water on three sides. We looked through a mounted telescope to zero in on a flat-bottomed fishing boat anchored in the pond. Another boat, with its rear deck filled with wooden traps, motored across the water.

I walked down to a thin beach, covered in shells and pebbles. An angler from Worcester, Massachusetts, pulled on waders and walked 15 feet into the pond to fly-cast for stripers.

After a break, we retraced our steps to a trail junction and took a left on the Cross Refuge Trail through what's called a glacial outwash plain. The flat ground is east of the Charlestown Moraine, a long ridgeline created during the Ice Age, and was formed when retreating glaciers deposited a rich, rock-free, silt-loam soil. In the fertile ground, Native Americans planted corn, beans, squash, pumpkins, and tobacco used for medicines and ceremonies.

At several sites in Ninigret, archeologists have found remnants of Native American life, including "middens," or refuse heaps that contained oyster, quahog, mussel, razor clam and scallop shells, as well as some quartz and pieces of pottery.

In the 1600s, Colonial farmers pushed out the Native Americans. One area of Ninigret includes a 1-mile-wide parcel from Watchaug Pond to the

A fishing boat cruises Ninigret Pond in the Ninigret National Wildlife Refuge in Charlestown.

ocean that the king of England granted to Jeffrey Champlin. By the 1700s, the land had become a 2,000-acre plantation, and under the ownership of Christopher Champlin, 200 slaves tended more than 600 sheep, 50 dairy cows and hundreds of pigs. Cheese, ham, and wool were shipped to Newport, New York, Europe and the West Indies.

By the 1800s, the land was divided into dairy, sheep, and pig farms. The owners planted corn and hay, mainly to feed the livestock. Seaweed was also sold as crop fertilizer.

The land stayed largely undeveloped until the Navy acquired the Hunter Harbor summer colony and 588 acres of farmland in 1942. After World War II, the base was used as a practice aircraft carrier landing field for anti-submarine planes that flew from Quonset Airfield.

In 1970, the Navy transferred the land to the U.S. Fish and Wildlife Service, which created the refuge.

As the trail leads through chapters of Rhode Island history, we followed the path through heavy woods filled with the sights and sounds of warblers, sparrows, and finches. We also sniffed the sweet smell of honeysuckle.

Eventually, we came to an intersection, with a break left to a fishing area.

We went straight and passed through some wooded swamps until spotting Foster's Cove through some trees on the left. Past a bench built as an Eagle Scout project, I walked down a side path to survey the cove and noted the Willows Inn across the water. At one time, pontoon planes landed on the cove to bring guests to the summer retreat.

We followed a sign for the Charlietown Runway Trail and took the paved path on a long strip of asphalt to the entrance of the Ninigret National Wildlife Refuge. We then returned to where we parked.

After spending the early spring hiking inland trails, I decided it was time to visit the ocean and picked Ninigret. I was surprised to find all the naval and farming history. That was a bonus to the unique walk to the coastal pond that every Rhode Islander can enjoy.

Challenging Hikes

Long Pond can be seen from a rocky trail that runs along a ledge above the water.

31   Long Pond Woods

Meet the sparkling blue star of Wes Anderson's film "Moonrise Kingdom"

Distance: 4.5 miles
Time: 3.5 hours
Difficulty: Strenuous climbs over ridges; moderate in hilly areas; easy on flat sections

Access: Off I-95, take Exit 4 from Rte. 3 and turn northwest on Canonchet Road. Drive about 1.5 miles and take a left on Stubtown Road to the trailhead on the right.
Parking: Available for a few cars
Dogs: Allowed in state-owned areas but not allowed on Audubon properties
Last Date Hiked: April 2021
Trailhead GPS: 41.50022, -71.76033

HOPKINTON—Ice-split glacial boulders. Ledges as smooth as tabletops that run from the hillside to the shore. A narrow, rock-walled "cathedral" with stone steps that climb to a hemlock ceiling.

Those are just a few of the sights in Long Pond Woods Wildlife Refuge.

But what really caught the eye of filmmakers was a massive outcropping with a high perch and views of the full length of Long Pond. That's the scene that gave the 2012 Wes Anderson movie "Moonrise Kingdom" a special Rhode Island look.

Twice before, I had hiked through the strenuous, up-and-down terrain on a trail that edges three ponds. But this time, I paid more attention to the natural beauty of the landscape as a perfect setting for a movie about two youngsters trying to find their way out of tough lives.

I set out from a small lot on Stubtown Road in the state-owned Rockville Management Area on a segment of the 22-mile Narragansett Trail which runs northwest and into the Pachaug Forest in Connecticut.

The yellow-blazed trail starts out through an old picnic ground with a decaying shelter and follows a rocky and at times muddy path along the west bank of the 30-acre Ashville Pond. There are stream crossings and side spurs to fishing spots.

Long Pond Woods

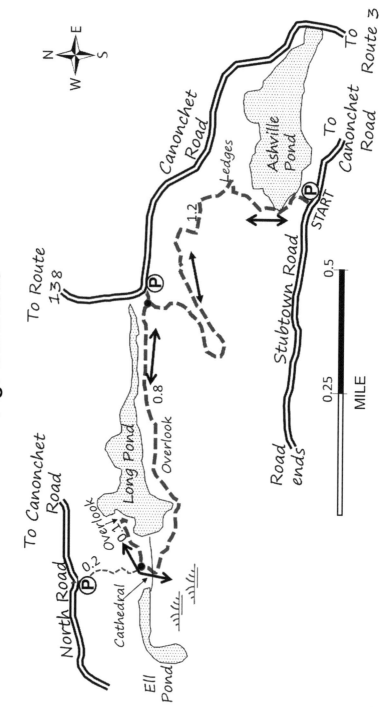

The trail soon opens to a long, flat ledge, with water running over it, that extends down to the pond. When I hiked this area last winter, ice covered the trail.

The ledges, called Table Rock, were wet but not frozen on this late April morning. I turned left and north to follow the yellow blazes across the ledge and through a stone wall. In a short distance, the path passes through stone enclosures at strange angles, piles of rocks and a large boulder field. You have to wonder who could have farmed here.

The trail meanders through mountain laurel tunnels and under oaks before reaching a trailhead and parking lot off Canonchet Road.

I turned west and stayed on the yellow-blazed trail to enter the 220-acre Long Pond Woods Wildlife Refuge, managed by the Audubon Society and The Nature Conservancy. The path ran along a long ledge with a parallel stone wall on the higher ground on the left. There were some good views to the right into the deep ravine with a brook running through it. I heard spring frogs trilling in the wetlands below and a woodpecker drumming on the far bank. Through the trees, you can see Long Pond and a pair of private cottages on the opposite shore.

The trail gets much tougher from here on, with steep climbs and scrambles up and down rocks, ledges, and outcroppings. There's a short section of wooden stairs built by scouts. After a little more than a mile, the trail reaches the western end of Long Pond and crosses a boardwalk. The best parts are just ahead.

Hikers enter a "cathedral"—a steep, deep, and narrow natural cleft cut between high rock walls on both sides. Exposed stones in the trail create a rocky stairway that rises under the shade of towering hemlocks. It's a rewarding climb.

At the top, hikers have a choice. They can continue north on the yellow-blazed trail to North Road. Or, an unblazed path west that's a little hard to find takes you to an overgrown outlook above Ell Pond, named for the "L" shape. The National Park Service placed a bronze plaque there in 1974 to designate it as a national natural landmark.

I went right and east on an unmarked path, down into a hollow, and then up the other side to reach an immense outcropping and the enchanting view from "Moonrise Kingdom." I avoided the granite-faced cliffs to

The perch on a massive outcropping offers a stunning view of Long Pond, where scenes from the movie "Moonrise Kingdom" were filmed.

the right and circled to the left of the huge rock formation before using my hands to climb up a crevice to reach the top. Long Pond is below, and the sparkling blue water —ringed by budding trees—narrows and stretches east for quite a distance. The wide-angle view from the overlook is spectacular.

Looking south across the pond, you can see the tough terrain I crossed to get there. I stood on the spot where the camera must have been placed to film the campsite where the 12-year-old runaways, Suzy and Sam, rested for a night. Other scenes in "Moonrise Kingdom" were shot farther north and just off the Narragansett Trail at Yawgoog Scout Reservation, and around Narragansett Bay on Conanicut and Prudence Islands, and in Newport.

After enjoying the view, eating a snack for energy and drinking some water, I retraced my steps and headed back on the same trail. The rigorous terrain tired me out, and I stopped several times to catch my breath before eventually returning to where I started.

If you want a shorter hike, it's about 1.2 miles from the Stubtown Road lot to the Canonchet Road trailhead, and it's about a mile from there to the western edge of Long Pond. You can also start from North Road and hike south to Long Pond, but that trail is steep, rocky and fairly rigorous.

Whichever way you choose, there are many interesting features to see along the trails. But the view from the perch above Long Pond is special, whether you see it in person or on the screen.

Parris Brook tumbles alongside the Mount Tom Trail in the Arcadia Management Area in Exeter.

32 Mount Tom Trail

Deep into the woods, a reforested wonder

Distance: 7 miles
Time: 3.5 hours
Difficulty: Moderate to challenging on rocky trials and ridges

Access: Off Route 3, drive west on Route 165 for 2.5 miles to a small turnout on the left with a sign "Appie Crossing."
Parking: Available for a few cars
Dogs: Allowed, but must be leashed
Last Date Hiked: January 2021
Trailhead GPS: 41.57665, -71.70374

EXETER—The Wood River winds gently for miles through a dense forest in the Arcadia Management Area in South County. It's hard to believe that 70 years ago a wildfire burned and scarred 8,000 acres of timberland around the river.

But a forward-thinking reforestation project planted 690,000 seedlings that have grown into thick stands of pine, beech and oak and regenerated one of the finest hiking and recreation areas in Rhode Island. That's a lesson in recovering from a crisis that seems especially pertinent after the pandemic swept through Rhode Island.

I set out to explore the river and surrounding woods from a small turnout off Route 165 called Appie Crossing. I headed west on the white-blazed Mount Tom Trail that rose and fell easily with the terrain. I crossed Summit Road, and in about a mile, I reached the banks of the Wood River and a sturdy footbridge. Before it was built by the Appalachian Mountain Club in 2015, hikers waded across the river or walked to a cement bridge on 165 and then back to the trail.

From the middle of the new bridge, I've looked upstream in different seasons and studied fly fishermen casting for trout, salmon and char. And downstream, I've watched kayakers and canoeists put in at a calm stretch of the river. Today, all is quiet. Not a soul around.

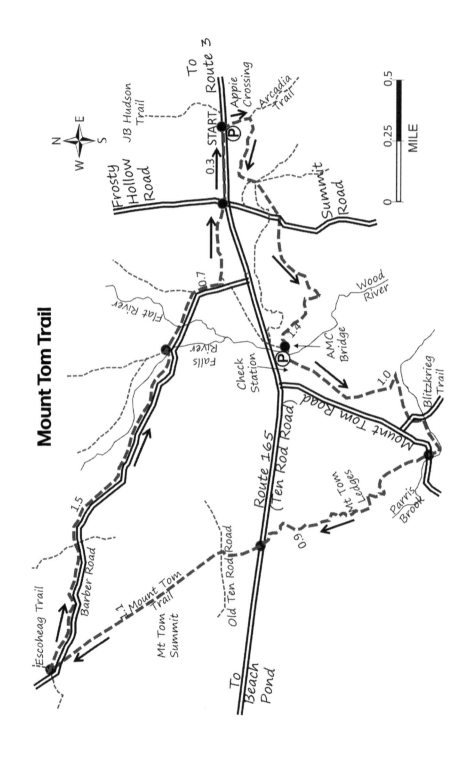

On the other side of the river, I walked by a picnic shelter and checking station, where hunters in various seasons must report. I headed back into the woods, picked up the white-blazed trail and noted a sign warning of timber harvesting in the area.

Twenty years ago, a forest mitigation program in this part of the woods thinned some old, chipped and knocked-down trees. Now, there's a stretch of smaller, bright green pines growing among tall, ramrod-straight white pines.

The path is wide and soft with pine needles. It's comforting.

The trail leads to a dirt road. To shorten your hike, retrace your steps or turn right and follow the road to Route 165 and return to where you started. There's a wide berm but stay far off the road to be safe.

I continued across the road on the white-blazed Mount Tom Trail for the most interesting part of the hike that runs along Parris Brook. There's a series of cascades over small dams, some man-made to create pools and fast-rushing water to enhance trout fishing. The trail soon leaves the brook and climbs, sometimes steeply, over rocks to ledges with views to the southwest. As you hike higher, the trail turns west along a rocky ridgeline for about a quarter mile, with plenty of steep cliffs that offer great vistas. I once saw hawks soaring above the trees.

On one stretch along the exposed ledges, hikers may be surprised to find three stone thrones, erected anonymously, that face west. It must be beautiful to sit there and watch the sunset, but not today, because I still have miles to go before I rest.

The rocky trail goes down, up and over ridges and around boulders before reaching Route 165 and continues on the other side of the road. Be careful, as cars quickly approach over the crest of the hill.

The trail rises up the hillside for a short distance and starts to level off before crossing Old Ten Rod Road. Hikers should stay on the white-blazed trail to cross the 460-foot Mount Tom, although you won't know it because there are no views and no real summit.

After that, the trail continues flat and rutted from bikers and hikers. I walked over frozen mud, but in wet weather, water sometimes runs down the path.

Just off the trail, there's a wide stretch of downed trees and brush that were defoliated by spongy moths a few years ago. The Rhode Island Department

The Wood River flows south under the Appalachian Mountain Club Bridge along the Mount Tom Trail in the Arcadia Management Area.

of Environmental Management is timber harvesting to remove swaths of dead oak and other trees, called snags, that could fuel wildfires.

The scene made me think of the scarring from the 1951 wildfire, the replanting and the constant need to manage and preserve the forest. The work being done now will benefit future generations of Rhode Islanders.

The white-blazed trail runs to Barber Road. I turned right and east on the hard-packed gravel road that in one section is part of the blue-blazed North South Trail. On the left are some game and forest management areas, where DEM stocks pheasants and grows grasses and cover crops. Hikers pass through mostly closed gates to keep vehicles off the road. Horses are allowed, so watch where you step. There are also some shaded side cuts to adjacent streams where horses and riders can rest.

I crossed a bridge over the Falls River, which flows from Stepstone Falls to the northwest, and then another one over the Flat River. The two rivers merge to form the Wood River, which runs through the heart of Arcadia and for 20 miles before converging with the Pawcatuck River. The rivers in 2019 were included in the National Wild and Scenic Rivers System, providing access to federal funds to protect and enhance the 300-square-mile watershed.

From the gravel road, a blue-blazed trail opens on the left that runs through the woods and leads you back to Route 165. If you miss it, stay on the road to return to Route 165.

The Mount Tom Trail in the 14,000-acre Arcadia, the state's largest recreation area, is a long and at times rigorous hike. Wear sturdy footwear with solid soles and at least 200 square inches of orange during hunting seasons. Bring plenty of water, keep a good map handy and pay attention to the trail markers.

Then, enjoy one of the finest deep-wood hikes in Rhode Island.

Pine Swamp Brook flows under a bridge and cascades over rocks to form a small, refreshing waterfall.

33 Parker Woodland Wildlife Refuge

Where the mystery of stone cairns remains unsolved

Distance: 4.5 miles
Time: 2 hours
Difficulty: Moderate to challenging, with some rocky, rooted trails and climbs over ledges

Access: Off Route 95, take Route 102 north into Coventry. Turn right on Maple Valley Road to a lot on the left
Parking: Available at the trailhead
Dogs: Not allowed
Last Date Hiked: June 2021
Trailhead GPS: 41.71677, -71.69811

COVENTRY—The remains of Caleb Vaughn's farm give hikers a good look at Colonial life in Rhode Island 250 years ago.

The farmhouse's rock-lined foundation includes rubble from a center chimney that was once used for cooking, baking, and heating. Nearby, large, flat field stones were laid to support timbers that held up the roof of a barn. Stone walls run in all directions on the hillside to separate pastures, woodlots, and orchards. Some of them penned livestock.

While the Vaughn site offers clear evidence of the early settlers, there's a mystery on the other side of the property, where dozens of cairns have been erected. Nobody is sure who built them, when or why. (More later.)

The structures are all in the George B. Parker Woodland Wildlife Refuge and are linked by trails that cross cascading streams, wind around huge, glacial boulders and climb three sets of ledges and outcroppings that make for a good workout.

The 860-acre preserve was part of the 1642 Shawomet Purchase that the colonists made from the Narragansetts. Over the centuries, the land was inhabited by the Watermans, Vaughns, Goffs and then by George Parker, who deeded some of the land in 1941 to the Audubon Society of Rhode Island, which later expanded and still manages the refuge.

Parker Woodland Wildlife Refuge

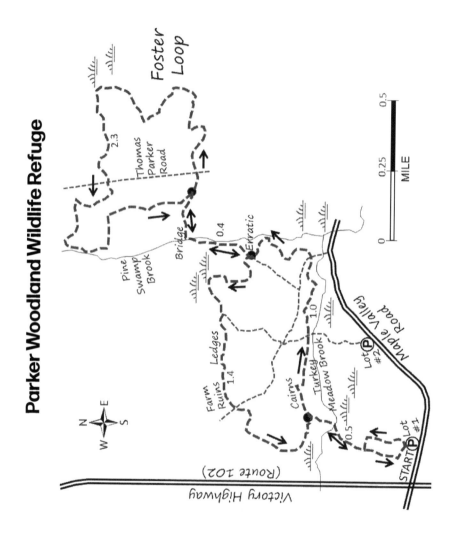

The remains of a farmhouse built by the Vaughn family 250 years ago is just one of the draws for history buffs at the George B. Parker Woodland Wildlife Refuge in Coventry.

I set out from a trailhead off Maple Valley Road with a friend on a humid early morning with temperatures rising into the 90s.

We followed the orange-blazed trail down a long slope and crossed boardwalks and walkways over forested wetlands covered with ferns, skunk cabbage and red maples. We also walked over a small bridge that spans Turkey Meadow Brook.

At a junction, we went right on the blue-blazed Paul Cook Memorial Trail and hiked upland along a heavily rooted path, with the brook running parallel and below us.

The trail then meanders through a curiosity—dozens of well-built, cone-shaped cairns about 3 to 5 feet tall that are scattered in the woods.

Archeologists have studied the rock formations but aren't sure who built them.

Some say the Narragansetts crafted the cairns to mark ceremonial spots. Others say pre-Colonial Celtic people put up the monuments. Early farmers sometimes created rock piles to mark points along stone walls and

The origins of dozens of well-crafted stone cairns, built in no apparent pattern, remain a mystery to archeologists.

property lines, but the cairns are in no apparent pattern, and the land is so rocky and filled with boulders that it's doubtful farmers tried to use it. So, the mystery continues.

Back on the trail headed east, a side path under red oaks, maples and a few birches opens on the right, crosses a bridge over slow-moving Turkey Meadow Brook and leads to another parking lot. But what's more interesting are several large, earth-covered mounds. Historians agree they are the residue of stacks of hardwoods that were fired to make charcoal—a process that developed into a local industry in the late 18th and early 19th centuries.

We walked back to the blue-blazed trail and crossed wide, grassy Biscuit Hill Road. Local legend says the cart path was named during the Revolutionary War after a wagon loaded with biscuits and headed for General Rochambeau's army turned over, spilling bread across the hillside.

At that point, the trail then turns north, leaving Turkey Meadow Brook that flows south by the remains of a sawmill that ran from the 1760s to 1875.

The path leads to a trail junction and a huge, glacial erratic left from the Ice Age. We turned right on the yellow-blazed trail that ran downhill and then along Pine Swamp Brook. We stopped at a bridge above a cascade that had sculpted the rocks below and formed a small, tumbling waterfall. It was refreshing.

It was too hot to continue east on what's called the Foster Loop, which runs for 2.5 miles. But on prior hikes along the Milton A. Gowdey Memorial Trail, I've seen Colonial-era stone quarries, crossed Pig Hill Road under white pines and sat on a large, flat table rock reportedly shaped by the Narragansetts.

We returned to the glacial erratic and turned right on the blue-blazed trail that climbed a hillside and several ledges that had me huffing and puffing. After several switchbacks that passed through and around ice-split boulders, the path flattened under pine trees.

Crossing Biscuit Hill Road again, we continued to the remains of the farm site that Caleb Vaughn purchased in 1760, which includes evidence of a deep, stone-lined well, gardens and an orchard.

The trail then passes near more stone walls before descending slowly to a boardwalk over wetlands and then to the junction with the orange trail. We headed back and took a jog to the right, edging a meadow that is cut every fall to preserve a natural habitat for nesting birds and wildlife. Birdhouses in the field attract Eastern bluebirds and tree swallows.

From there, it was a few more steps back to the car.

I drove home, tired but still thinking about the mystery. While everybody these days seems to be fascinated by unidentified objects in the sky, I'm more interested in earthbound curiosities, including who built those rock cairns, and why.

Hikers from Rhode Island, Connecticut and Massachusetts gather at the Tri-State Marker, the only point where the three states meet.

34 Tri-Town Marker / Buck Hill Management Area

On the hunt for the spot where 3 neighbors converge

Distance: 6 miles
Time: 3 hours
Difficulty: Moderate on rocky trails

Access: Take Route 100 northwest about 5.3 miles out of Pascoag and turn left on Buck Hill Road. Drive 2.3 miles and take a right for 0.3 miles to a gate.
Parking: Available at the trailhead
Dogs: Allowed
Last Date Hiked: April 2021
Trailhead GPS: 41.98384, -71.78970

BURRILLVILLE—The Tri-State Marker, a granite obelisk at the only point where Rhode Island, Connecticut, and Massachusetts meet, attracts hikers from throughout the region.

When I visited on an early April morning, a family from Connecticut had walked in from the west. A couple from Massachusetts had hiked from the north.

I arrived from the east after crossing the 2,000-acre Buck Hill Management Area. Along the way, I examined an impressive earthen dam that held back a massive wildlife and waterfowl marsh. I inspected well-preserved stone foundations and cellar holes built by early farmers. I followed, with one foot in Rhode Island and the other in Massachusetts, a series of small, stone pillars that lead to the Tri-State Marker.

Finding the obelisk, erected in 1883 to settle border disputes, was a highlight of the hike through the preserve managed by the Rhode Island Department of Environmental Management and tucked into the far northwest corner of the state.

I put on a required orange vest because it was hunting season and set out from a gate at the end of a parking area. I walked down a gravel road with a small, reed-filled pond on the left.

Tri-Town Marker / Buck Hill Management Area

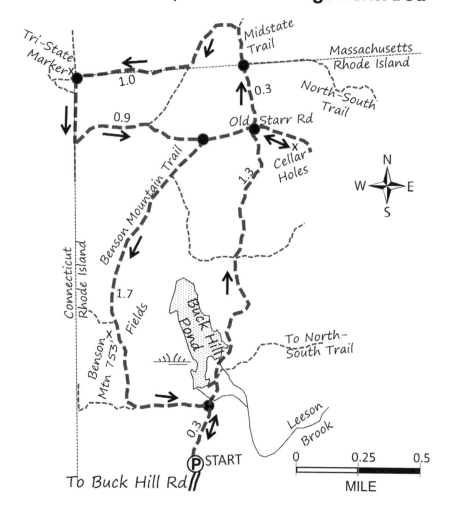

In a third of a mile, the road ran through pines and crossed a bridge with Leeson Brook rushing underneath. There was some beaver activity downstream. I took a short side trail on the left to a 500-foot long, 13-foot-high dike built in 1962 to create a huge swamp.

A metal drain, installed in 2006, houses a water control system to manipulate the water levels to improve the habitat. In the spring, the water is lowered to allow vegetation to sprout and grow and give coverage to migrating waterfowl to forage. It also provides hunting opportunities.

Back on the trail, a side lane called Benson Mountain Road breaks to the east.

I stayed on the yellow-blazed path that narrows and heads north. An opening in the trees allows a look west at the marsh where hikers report seeing all types of waterfowl.

The trail gets rocky, rises under hemlocks and mountain laurel, and crosses a fire road. At about 1.5 miles from the start, the path intersects with Old Starr Road. I walked a few hundred yards east to find well-built stone enclosures and walls. The late naturalist Ken Weber reported in his trail posts that the area's first white settler may have lived here.

I returned to the yellow-blazed trail, and reached the state line, which is also the terminus of the North South Trail, where signs offer several options, including a walk 2.1 miles east to Wallum Lake.

I hiked a short distance north on the Midstate trail, which runs through the Douglas State Forest in Massachusetts. Then, I turned southwest to a trail along the state border to head for the Tri-State Marker. At the intersection, there are larger stone foundations with the remains of center chimneys.

Along the trail, three small stone posts etched with "RI" on one side and "Mass" on the other guide the route over rolling terrain.

After a long, gradual rise, the trail crests on a knoll just above a circular clearing, within sight of the Tri-State Marker and other hikers. I noticed a youngster trying to climb the four-foot pillar.

The four-sided obelisk is sunk five feet deep and has a six-inch pyramid top. State abbreviations—RI facing east, Conn facing west and Mass facing north—are carved on three sides. The fourth side is blank. The pillar was put up to try to resolve a series of border disputes, some of which landed

A man-made earthen dike holds back water in a massive wildlife and waterfowl marsh in the Buck Hill Management Area in Burrillville.

in state supreme courts, that date to the Colonial days. The governments of Massachusetts and Rhode Island formed a commission to study land deeds, documents, and other records to set the border.

Connecticut didn't sign onto the original agreement, so while "1883" is carved under the RI and Mass abbreviations, Connecticut's side does not include the date.

After a few minutes of mulling over this convergence of neighbors, I headed south along the Rhode Island/Connecticut line and found a trail on the left with water running over it. Look closely to see a slab marker with "RI" on one side and "C" on the other side. I took that trail east, up a long gradual slope.

At a fork, I stayed right on a road over a ridge on Benson Mountain (753 feet and named for a family that lived there) and noted several side roads into clear-cut fields. DEM workers mow the fields twice a year to promote more diverse plants, limit the intrusion of woody vegetation and provide a habitat for grassland nesting birds and pollinators. During the spring and summer and small game season, the fields are stocked with ring-necked pheasants.

I followed the road as it eventually bent east, spotted the swamp through the trees, and returned to the trail where I started. After a quick right, I was back at the lot.

The state-owned preserve is shared by hunters, birders, hikers, and walkers out to explore the outdoors.

There's a lot to see and learn. But my favorite stop was the Tri-State Marker—a unique destination and worth a hike to see for yourself.

The Walkabout Trail, cut in 1965 by Australian sailors while their ship was in drydock in Newport, starts at the beach in the George Washington Management Area in Glocester.

The trail runs from Glocester into Burrillville and passes by quiet Wilbur Pond.

35 Walkabout Trail / George Washington Management Area

Retracing an Aussie "Walkabout"

Distance: 8.2 miles
Time: 4 hours
Difficulty: Moderate, with rocky paths, some hills and wetlands

Access: Drive 4.5 miles west on Route 44 from Chepachet to the entrance for the George Washington Management Area on the right.
Parking: Available for a few cars at a small turnout on the left side of the entrance road
Dogs: Allowed, but must be leashed
Last Date Hiked: July 2001
Trailhead GPS: 41.92394, -71.75832

GLOCESTER—Australian sailors cut the Walkabout Trail in 1965 while their ship, the HMAS Perth, was in dry dock in Newport.

The Aussies spent a month laying out the trail after the Rhode Island Division of Forestry asked for their help during the development of the 4,000-acre George Washington Management Area.

In return, the trail was named Walkabout, a reference to the Australian aborigines' rite of passage, during which young males wander the wilderness for months to learn about the land, spirits and their ancestors and make the transition into manhood.

The sailors created a challenging network of trails around ponds, under hemlock forests, through marshlands, across streams, up and down rocky hillsides and by glacial boulders. When I recently retraced the sailors' steps, I was impressed by their work.

Two hiking buddies, George and Rick, and I set out by walking down a short road with a headquarters building on the left that was built by the Civilian Conservation Corps, the federal jobs program set up in the 1930s.

The trailhead is at the beach on Bowdish Reservoir. There's a marker

Walkabout Trail / George Washington Management Area

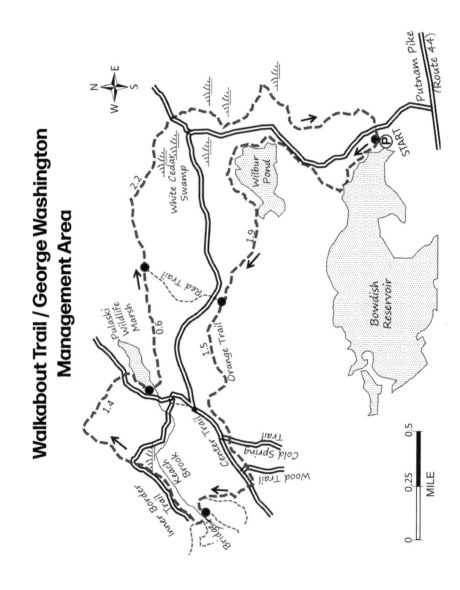

with an old gate crank and a plaque noting that the original dam that created the pond was built in 1883. The gate mechanism was removed in May 2001 during the reconstruction of the dam on the opposite side of the 226-acre reservoir.

A bog once encompassed the site, and hikers report still seeing bog mats—small, vegetated islands called sphagnum moss—floating in 7 feet of water near the center of the pond. You can't walk on them without falling through.

At the trailhead, three loops start at the same point: blue, 1.6 miles; red, 4.8 miles; and orange, 8 miles. We decided on the orange-blazed trail, which also includes a segment of the blue-blazed North South Trail that runs for 78 miles from Charlestown to Burrillville. Volunteers installed brown signs along the North South Trail with mileage and GPS positions to help first responders locate hikers in an emergency.

The start of the path hugs the shoreline of the reservoir, where the 300 Australians who built the trail swam after long days of toil. We saw some campsites on the right along a gravel camp road and side paths to rocky points jutting into the reservoir.

The trail continued through some dense woodlands and wetlands, some with wooden bridges. One is etched with a quote. "Life is a Path."

Crossing from Glocester into Burrillville, we walked along the banks of the tranquil and picturesque Wilbur Pond. We rousted a large hawk (maybe an osprey) that spread its wings and took flight.

At the northern end of a cove, we reentered the deep woods and headed west under pine trees and mountain laurel. The red trail broke off to the north, but we continued west around moss-covered boulders and crossed three gravel roads: Cold Spring, Wood Trail and Center Trail. Many cross-country ski trails intersected with the path. One of them leads west to Peck Pond in adjacent Casimir Pulaski Park.

The orange-blazed trail turns north and down a long, gentle slope under a shady hemlock grove. We reached a wide, well-built bridge over Keach Brook and spent some time there studying the construction. The bridge is part of the Old Winter Recreation Trails Program and was built sturdy enough to allow snowmobiles to groom trails for cross-country skiing.

After the bridge, the path turned sharply east and ran parallel with the Inner Border Trail before passing through the Pulaski wildlife marshes. There were signs of beaver activity, and the path at times turned muddy and rocky. Finding good footing became a bit of a chore.

The trail continues along the banks of a shallow pond held back by a long, grassy, exposed earthen dam. Hikers report seeing swallows, kingfishers and wood ducks in the water, as well as muskrats and beavers.

· We crossed the dam, climbed a small hill, and then descended to White Cedar Swamp, walking across dozens of short logs placed side by side to create an old-fashioned corduroy road.

There was another set of ups and downs before the trail flattened, reached an intersection with the Blue Trail on the right and then returned to the spot where we started.

I walked around the trailhead and a weathered plaque that noted that the trail was named and constructed by personnel of Her Majesty's Ship Perth during Operation Black Swan in June 1965. It's a nice reminder of the great work our Aussie friends did.

Thanks, mates.

36 Escoheag Trail / Ben Utter Trail / Stepstone Falls

The journey to it is as spectacular as its tumbling water

Distance: 6 miles
Time: 3 hours
Difficulty: Moderate, with some rocky ridges and stream crossings

Access: Off Route 165 west, take Escoheag Hill Road north for one mile to the trailhead by an old cabin.
Parking: Available in a lot
Dogs: Allowed, but must be leashed
Last Date Hiked: April 2022
Trailhead GPS: 41.58998, -71.75783

EXETER—Stepstone Falls, a series of tumbling cascades over a terrace of flat, smooth stones, is an impressive, unique feature in the Arcadia Management Area.

Every Rhode Islander should make multiple trips to experience the falls in different seasons. In the spring, the Falls River gushes and crashes over the rocks, creating a low rumble. But in dry summers, the water trickles quietly downstream over the stone steps.

Don't just drive down Falls River Road to the bridge just above the falls—hike there. The journey can be as interesting, educational, and fun as the destination.

Our son, Daniel, and I set out for the falls from Escoheag Hill Road by a small, boarded-up cabin built by the Civilian Conservation Corps (CCC) in the 1930s. We walked by a barred gate at the entrance of Plain Road and went a short distance to the right and down another gravel lane that was lined with a stone drainage ditch. The channel was also built by young CCC workers who stayed at the nearby Escoheag/Beach Pond Camp.

The path makes a loop, and at the far end, a trailhead marks the start of the Escoheag Trail. Escoheag is a Native American term for "origin of

Escoheag Trail / Ben Utter Trail / Stepstone Falls

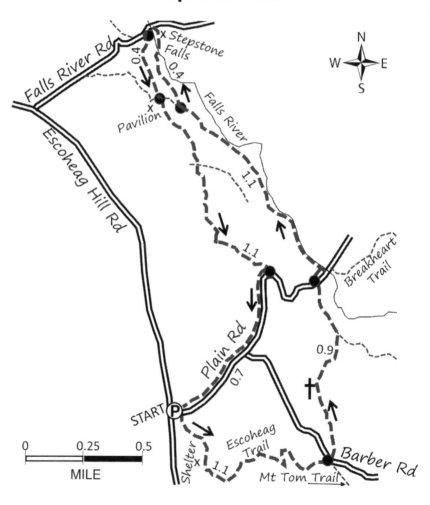

three rivers." We took the white-blazed path by some large boulders and spotted on the right the roofline of a shelter on a high outcropping. A side path led to a stone-sided and floored pavilion, originally built by the CCC and restored in 2011 by the Rhode Island Trials Club, a motorbike organization. The shelter was once a destination in the Ledges Picnic Area, a popular spot for weekend visitors. But it seemed to be abandoned, and we found little evidence of any picnic tables or fireplaces.

Back on the trail, the path runs down a ridge and across several small brooks, some with wooden bridges and others requiring some hops across the rocks. The trail winds through the hollow under beech and oak trees and over other streams before crossing more ridges.

At one point, the trail runs along the base of low cliffs before climbing to the top of a ledge. The path crosses some flat ground before reaching a ridgeline where the oak trees had been devastated in 2016 and 2017 by a spongy moth caterpillar infestation and drought. The Rhode Island Department of Environmental Management has cleared many of the dead trees, but some remain.

The trail continues down a hillside before intersecting with Barber Road. The Mount Tom Trail breaks off to the right, but we stayed straight on the white-blazed trail and passed on the left an overgrown cemetery with small, unmarked gravestones. The trail then slopes downhill to a wide, pine-needle covered path that merges with the blue-blazed North South Trail.

We followed the path to Plain Road, took a right and walked 100 yards to the Falls River, which flows southeast to the Wood River. A bridge over the river has been rebuilt with horizontal steel beam supports, but the old stone supports are still visible under the bridge.

On the other side of the bridge is the Breakheart Trail and Penny Hill to the northeast.

We turned left before the bridge to pick up the yellow-blazed Ben Utter Trail, named for a pioneer of the state's trail network. The path follows the river upstream and crosses several wooden bridges over tributaries of the clear, fast-running river. From the bank, we noted many mini-waterfalls, some natural and some man made by placing logs anchored by stones in the river.

The Falls River flows gently over a series of natural and man-made terraces to form Stepstone Falls, a popular hiking destination in the Arcadia Management Area.

A pavilion with stone sides, originally built by Civilian Conservation Corp workers in the 1930s, is at the center of the old Ledges Picnic Area.

The work creates pools below the small dams and provides good spots for trout fishing. Anglers report catching rainbow, brook, and brown trout there. I learned later that the DEM and the Narragansett Chapter of Trout Unlimited are studying the upper Wood River Watershed to form a plan to preserve the native fish and identify habitat-improvement projects that would enhance the area's pristine ecology.

As we walked, we also spotted the overgrown remains of an old grist mill on the left. Additional clues about how people made a living along the river were just ahead. We found an earthen dike that had been built to hold back water from a channel dug from the river. Below the impoundment, there's a millrace that funneled water to a stone foundation that once held a water wheel that ran a vertical sawmill. Water still seeped through the rocks that are now covered with thick, green moss.

Daniel and I continued on the trail until reaching a fork. The yellow-blazed path went left, but we turned right on the white-blazed River Trail, which crossed a rocky and at times muddy section crossed by several streams.

The Ben Utter Trail crosses wooden bridges that span tributaries of the fast-flowing Falls River.

After a bit, we reached a wide footbridge with railings that spanned the Falls River. Looking upstream, we could see Stepstone Falls. After the bridge, the path turns left and follows the east side of the river by piles of huge granite blocks left from a quarrying operation, now long abandoned.

We stopped at a low granite overlook to watch the river flow downstream over Stepstone Falls. Some logs and branches had been carried downstream during high water seasons and caught on the rocks. I tried to count the number of terraces that form the waterfalls but lost track while listening to the dull roar of the falls.

We walked to a bridge, crossed the river, and walked down the west bank just a short distance to a flat plateau of granite where visitors sit to watch the falls. Some of the stones that form the terraces seemed natural, but others appear to have been cut during the quarrying operation. There was also a rope swing that hung from an oak and could carry swimmers over a pool between the falls.

After a break and a snack while sitting at the edge of a waterfall, we headed back south on the yellow-blazed trail but took a detour on the right to climb stone steps uphill to a path to another abandoned picnic area. We saw a shed that perhaps covered a pumphouse, a stone water fountain, tables, and fireplaces. There's also a pavilion originally built by CCC workers and renovated by the Appalachian Mountain Club. The structure has wooden beam rafters and large fireplaces on each end.

Past the picnic area, one path runs down to the river and retraces the yellow-blazed trail to Plain Road. We stayed straight, though, and walked south on what must have been the old road to the picnic ground. We reached Plain Road, turned right, and walked up a steep grade to return to the gate where we'd parked.

Stepstone Falls is a great memory.

But I'll recall the hike to get there as much as the swift-running water tumbling down the stone steps.

Five-foot tall grass and wildflowers cover the old parking lots at Pine Top Ski Area, which closed in 1981.

Metal brackets stick out of the ground and once supported pipes that sprayed and directed water to make snow on the slopes.

37 Pine Top

On the trails of once popular, now lost, ski slopes

Distance: 4 miles
Time: 2.5 hours
Difficulty: Moderate, with a steep climb up a hill

Access: Off Route 95, take Route 3 to Route 165 west. Drive 5.5 miles and take a right on Escoheag Hill Road. Take a right on Falls River Road and drive to Stepstone Falls.
Parking: Available for a few cars
Dogs: Allowed
Last Date Hiked: August 2021
Trailhead GPS: 41.61274, -71.76060

WEST GREENWICH—Pine Top, the ski area on the slopes of Escoheag Hill, attracted tens of thousands of enthusiasts before closing in 1981.

That was before I arrived in Rhode Island, but over the years I've heard and read many stories about the once-popular recreation area. So, I set out on a hike in the remote, densely wooded area to search for what was left of Pine Top.

I found that little remains (more details later). Forty years after Pine Top shut down, the land has reclaimed most of what was once a busy destination for skiers and others out for some exercise and a good time.

I set out with fellow hikers George and Rick to find Pine Top, starting from Stepstone Falls to the south and following a segment of the blue-blazed North South Trail, which runs 78 miles from Charlestown to Burrillville.

The wide, well-marked trail started out flat and may have been a road, but it was wet and muddy in spots. Several times, the path was rerouted around standing water, a breeding ground for mosquitoes.

Through the trees on the right, we caught glimpses of the Falls River, which flows parallel to the trail on the east. Stone walls run on both sides of the path.

At one point, the trail cuts through a hillside, with rocks and boulders

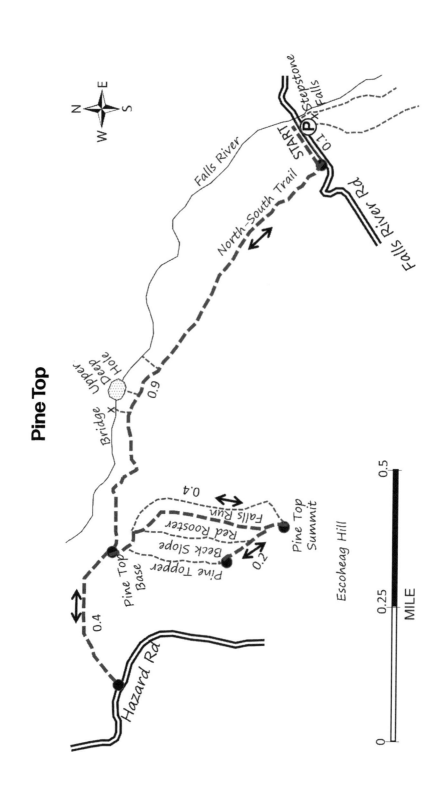

on the upslope on the left and a bush-covered downslope to the river on the right.

Then the trail bends west through the northwest section of the Arcadia Management Area and turns sandy through some huge fields. These were Pine Top's parking lots that held up to 1,200 cars. We meandered through the fields to a gate and the old entrance to Pine Top on Hazard Road, also known as Molasses Hill Road to the north and Escoheag Hill Road to the south. There are no signs to mark the ski area.

The North South Trail continued across the road. We retraced our steps, looking for an opening in the 5-foot grass and bushes for a trail to the bottom of Pine Top. We couldn't find one or see any signs of the base camp, lodge or ski runs in the trees at the foot of the hill.

After walking a few hundred yards through the fields, a trail opened on the right. We took it south and started to climb Escoheag Hill. Several side paths broke off the trail, but we stayed on the rutted route that looked like an old road or ski run.

Just off the trail, on a side path, we found a pile of debris from a collapsed wooden building that may have been a warming hut, a cabin for circuit breakers or a ski patrol shelter. In the trees behind the rubble, we spotted several sets of rusted brackets to support snow-making guns, sticking out of the ground and pointing west where the trials must have been.

We stayed on the side trail and, looking downhill, spotted what may have been what's left of the Falls Run ski trail. The other runs were Red Rooster, Beck Slope and Pine Topper. Skiers took off from near the 580-foot summit of Escoheag Hill and skied down 280 feet to the base.

We walked west and came to private property, a fence and a house in the distance. We turned south, walked a few more steps uphill and found four, huge cement blocks that anchored one of the two T-bars that brought skiers to the top. We saw no signs of the actual T-bar or flywheel or the two other rope tows that pulled up beginning skiers. We did see stands of pine trees that covered the area, and hence the name: Pine Top.

The ski area opened for the 1965-1966 season and was an immediate hit, especially for beginning skiers and others looking for a short drive to the ski slopes. The area is 20 miles southwest of Providence. Skiers paid $3.50 on weekdays ($4 on weekends) for a pine tree-shaped lift ticket. The

Four large cement blocks served as anchors for the T-bar that dropped skiers near the summit of Escoheag Hill.

lodge included a ski shop, a cafeteria, a small balcony bar and a lounge, where skiers warmed up and parents watched and waited for their kids.

At the time, Pine Top was one of several small local ski areas, including Yawgoo Valley in Exeter, Diamond Hill in Cumberland, Ski Valley in Cumberland, and Neutaconkanut Hill in Providence.

Most faded in popularity in the late 1970s after several bad snow years, victims of changing habits and interests and some tough economic times. Only Yawgoo remains.

Pine Top's owners tried to stay in business by opening a motorcycle course and a stop on the motocross circuit. But it wasn't enough, and Pine Top closed in 1981. Later in the decade, vandals set fire to the old ski lodge, burning it to the ground.

The state took over the land and the Rhode Island Department of Environmental Management, which manages the property, has no plans to change its wild and wooded terrain.

After completing our search, we hiked down the hill, stopping in one clearing for a gorgeous look into the valley below, and then walked back along the blue-blazed trail. We explored three short side trails to the Falls River.

One led to a relatively new bridge that crossed to a trail on the far side of the water. Another led to a widening of the river, called Upper Deep Hole. And the third led to an old well on the riverbank, with heavy-gauge vertical and horizontal pipes that may have been installed to draw and pump water up the hillside for snowmaking at Pine Top.

We ended our hike by returning to Stepstone Falls and rested by the cascading waterfalls.

On the drive home, I thought of all the people who had enjoyed Pine Top. Teenagers on their first date, beginners attending ski school and learning from a dozen instructors, the ski patrol monitoring the trails, workers flipping burgers in the cafeteria or pouring drinks in the bar and many others zooming down the slopes at night after a day of work or school or to enjoy an afternoon on a winter weekend.

All distant memories now, as Pine Top fades deeper into the landscape.

An engineering marvel of a stone slab bridge crosses a tributary of the Pawcatuck River.

38   Carolina Management Area

Looping north and south, flower-covered fields, wetlands, and dense woods

Distance: 7.5 miles
Time: 3.5 hours
Difficulty: Easy to moderate. Some flat roads, hills and wetlands

Access: Off Route 95, take Route 138 east. Turn south on Route 112 and drive for 2.5 miles to Pine Hill Road. Turn right and drive west for 1.5 miles to a checking station on the left.
Parking: Available at the trailhead
Dogs: Allowed, but must be leashed
Last Date Hiked: July 2021
Trailhead GPS: 41.48467, -71.66099

RICHMOND—Fields of wildflowers—purple loosestrife, goldenrod, tiger lilies, joe pye weed, black-eyed Susans and many others I couldn't identify—line the wide path that meanders through the Carolina Management Area.

The 2,350-acre property also includes an old stone bridge over a tributary of the Pawcatuck River, graveyards deep in the woods and an ancient, toppled beech tree that has served for decades as a landmark for hikers trying to navigate the isolated refuge.

The public, state-run management area has two loop trails—North and South—and both start near where Pine Hill Road crosses Meadow Brook.

I set out with two friends, George and Rick, from the Carolina South trailhead, located next to a tiny cemetery outlined with short granite posts and with gravestones that date back more than 125 years.

We walked on a gravel road to the left of a red cement-block hunters' check station and under tall pines with an overgrown field to the right. The path opens to acres of fields filled with grasses, weeds, and wildflowers. Two cyclists passed us, headed north.

The Department of Environmental Management's Division of Fish and Wildlife manages 42 fields on the property and works to increase food and

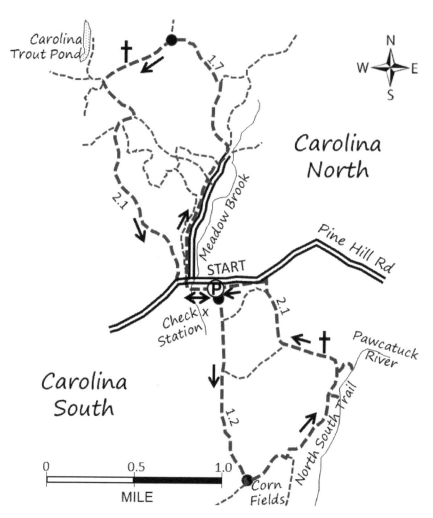

cover for game and nongame wildlife. The effort includes planting food and cover crops and periodically mowing the brush fields and pasture grasslands.

The DEM also stocks the fields with ring-necked pheasants in the fall.

The area is habitat for rabbits, gray squirrels, white-tailed deer, and furbearers such as racoons, coyote, muskrat and mink, according to the DEM. Game birds include ruffed grouse, wild turkeys, pheasants, woodcocks and bobwhites.

Along the trail, there are several side paths, including one on the left that leads to a cellar hole from an old farmhouse on the banks of Meadow Brook.

We continued on the main path through the fields, some lowlands covered with ferns and then to a T intersection. We walked up a hillside on the left to the edge of a huge field with row after row of corn. An elevated irrigation system was visible on the horizon.

From there, a narrow, almost overgrown path opens on the left and circles the perimeter of the field, with the remains of an old barn on the right.

Just after the barn ruins, there's a line of wooden posts marked with blue blazes for the North South Trail that runs north over the hill and south into the fields.

We went left and north into the forest and noticed plenty of shiny poison ivy just off the path. We also had to sidestep piles of horse droppings.

We took a short side spur that leads to an abandoned canoe camp on the Pawcatuck, with a fire ring and wooden bench hidden by heavy growth.

Farther down on the main trail, we followed another side path on the right to a wide, sturdy, stone slab bridge, supported by a vertical stone block that divided a tributary of the Pawcatuck into two channels. We studied the engineering work and pictured farmers driving their horses or oxen that pulled heavy carts loaded with crops.

Back on the main trail, we walked up a hillside and found an unusual cemetery enclosed by a picket fence. Usually, old graveyards are lined with stone walls. The plot is for members of the Kenyon family, and some headstones date to the 1700s.

Back on the main trail, the path flattened, straightened, and passed a clearing marked with a sign, "Harvested 2018." DEM thinned out 80 acres of diseased and over-mature, declining pines, part of a periodic harvesting

A wide trail along an old farm road through Carolina South cuts across acres of fields filled with wildflowers.

to keep the forest healthy by making it more resilient to pests and storms. The thinning also reduces fire risk and protects water quality.

A path into the clearing, called a skid trail, has been seeded, and hikers should stay off the trail while the plants take root. The new growth and felled trunks left behind help develop wildlife habitat and forest growth.

The trail exited on Pine Hill Road. We turned left, passed the lot where we parked and crossed Meadow Brook, where there's a knotted rope swing hanging from a tree above the water.

We turned right to start the Carolina North loop on a wide gravel road, called the Meadowbrook Trail, which is also a segment of the North South Trail. A side trail on the right ran down to Meadow Brook, a good trout-fishing stream.

After about a mile, with some fields on the left, the trail splits, with the North South trail headed to the right and the other trail, called Jerue Road, to the left. The trails are unmarked and unblazed, and we had to double-check our map.

We went left and northwest on a trail that at one point was blocked by a downed old beech tree that was once a landmark for hikers. The tree is carved with initials, some that go back more than 70 years. It's unclear what brought down the giant: age, insects, disease, a storm, or perhaps a strong wind.

No matter the cause, it's a sad passing.

Up ahead and just off the trail, lines of stone walls and animal pens from an old farm are visible under red and white oaks, maples, and pines. We explored and found a tiny, unmarked graveyard. Any lettering on the stones has disappeared with time and weather.

We noted but didn't take another trail that soon opens to the right and heads north to the popular Carolina Trout Pond, which the DEM stocks.

We crossed several other roads and side trails and pulled out the map again when we realized we were headed in the wrong direction. We retraced our steps and found what's called Shippee Road, which leads southeast to the Laurel Trail. The trail heads up and down hills and southwest for about half a mile until we returned to Pine Hill Road and our car.

In all, we hiked about four miles on Carolina South and another four miles on Carolina North over 3½ hours.

The Carolina trails seemed quieter and more remote than those in other state management areas. Because of that, my guess is that they are also more heavily used by hunters during the prime hunting seasons.

Many of the trails are flat roads, and if you enjoy a walk through flower-covered fields, acres of corn, wetlands, and dense woods—with also a bit of a challenge because of the unmarked trails—then Carolina should be on your mind.

The top of Rattlesnake Ledge offers a panoramic view of miles of unbroken forest in the Wickaboxet Management Area.

Caves at the base of Rattlesnake Ledge may have sheltered the Narragansetts during harsh winters.

39 Wickaboxet Management Area

Navigating Rhode Island's first state forest

Distance: 6 miles
Time: 3.5 hours
Difficulty: Easy to Moderate on flat trails and roads with some hills and downed trees

Access: Off Route 95, take Route 102 north and drive to Plain House Meeting Road. Take a left and drive three miles to a small lot on the right.
Parking: Available for several cars at the trailhead
Dogs: Allowed on a leash
Last Date Hiked: August 2021
Trailhead GPS: 41.63671, -71.73577

WEST GREENWICH—Rattlesnake Ledge and its view from the top of miles of unbroken forest were highlights of my recent hike through the Wickaboxet Management Area. I was also interested in the long history of the diverse people who walked the same trails centuries ago.

The Narragansetts once sheltered in the caves below the ledge when the tribe moved inland from the coast during winters. Wickaboxet is a Native American word for "near a small pond," and tiny Wickaboxet Pond is southwest of the preserve.

The Colonial farmers followed the Narragansetts and scratched out a living by raising crops on the thin, rocky soil. Many also raised livestock, which produced dairy products and meat.

Later, lumbermen harvested pines and hardwoods, and millers built factories on the streams as the economy shifted from agriculture to industry.

In 1932, Wickaboxet became Rhode Island's first state forest and a popular destination for picnics, hikes, and other outdoor recreation.

Today, Wickaboxet seems lost in time. The 678-acre state refuge is far less visited than the adjacent Tillinghast Pond Management Area or the Arcadia Management Area to the south. But I enjoyed the quiet hike

Wickaboxet Management Area

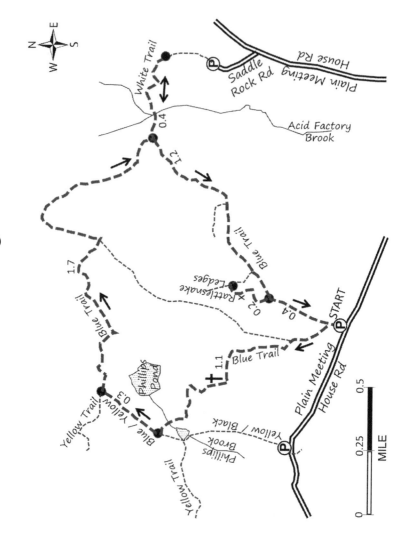

through deep woods. I traveled by boulder fields, over brooks and around ponds, while getting a good look into history.

I set out with George and Rick on a gravel road, perhaps an old farm lane, from the trailhead off Plain Meeting House Road. In less than 50 yards, the trail forked, and we went left on the blue-blazed Wickaboxet Loop Trail that is lined with bright green young pines. Just off the path on the right, we found, partially buried under leaves and brush, a stone-lined cellar hole from a farmhouse with a rectangular cut granite block for a threshold.

We continued under a mix of oaks, maples and pines, some planted after a huge fire in 1951 scarred the terrain. The path narrowed through dense ferns and then thorny raspberry bushes.

A little further ahead, we paused to explore the remains of the Wilcox Homestead, including several cellar holes, stone walls, pens, and animal runs. An unusual, large rectangular stone foundation had six stone steps leading upward. That's unusual, because most old farm houses have stone stairs leading down to the cellar.

Nearby, on a small hilltop, are the graves for members of the Wilcox family, with some dated from the early 1800s.

We rock-hopped over Phillips Brook, flowing south, and walked to an intersection with the wide, yellow-blazed Flintlock Trail at the eastern edge of the Tillinghast Pond Area. We took it north, with a slight detour on a side spur to a placid, lily-pad covered pond. The mosquitos kept us moving.

Returning to the main trail, we followed it to the opening of the blue-blazed trail on the right and climbed a small slope. As we descended on the other side, we walked through a giant boulder field with stones too big for the farmers to clear from the fields. We also had to navigate several downed trees that blocked the trail.

Just ahead, the path intersected with a white-blazed trail on the left. We took it into the Pratt Conservation Area, a 56-acre preserve managed by the West Greenwich Land Trust. The trail crossed over two plank bridges before reaching Acid Factory Brook, named for the Clapp family's mill that made acetic acid in the late 1880s for use in the textile mills.

We retraced our steps to the blue-blazed trail and hiked by the remains of the Matteson Homestead on a rocky, boulder-filled hillside. I spent some time thinking about how tough life must have been back then.

The remains of the Wilcox Homestead include stone steps that lead to a large foundation.

The path opened to a grassy lane, and we took it southwest, noting the high ledges that appeared off the trail to the north. In less than a mile, we took a side trail on the right to a huge, 50-foot outcropping, called Rattlesnake Ledge. The Narragansetts may have camped in the caves in the base during harsh winters. On the high, stony ridges, the Sachem held ceremonies.

Newer visitors have left graffiti.

A path curls to the back of the ledges and then up to the top, offering panoramic views of dense forest to the east, south and west. I couldn't see any buildings for miles around.

A hawk soared overhead, and the bushes were filled with tweeting birds. We saw no rattlesnakes but realized a misstep could result in a deadly fall.

After a rest, we returned to the main trail and passed the remains of a stone-lined well that may have been part of the old picnic grounds. From there, a short walk took us back to where we started.

Wickaboxet may be a lot less popular than it was in the past. But the quiet walk through its deep history and natural landscape gave me plenty to think about. That's a good hike.

40   Pachaug Trail

Roughing it among ledges, ravines, cliffs, and caves

Distance: 8 miles
Time: 4 hours
Difficulty: Moderate to challenging

Access: Off Route 95, take Route 3 in Exeter to Route 165 and drive 7 miles west to Beach Pond on the right.
Parking: Available at the Beach Pond lot. Some spots are reserved for boaters. There's a smaller lot across the road.
Dogs: Allowed, but must be leashed
Last Date Hiked: April 2021
Trailhead GPS: 41.57442, -71.78644

EXETER—I crossed the western border of Rhode Island in early April to hike a different type of trail than the farm lanes, cart paths and fire roads I'd been walking for the prior few weeks.

I found what I was looking for in the ledges, ravines, cliffs, caves, and clefts along the Pachaug Trail in Connecticut. Few settlers or farmers tried to make a living here. The rocky, rugged terrain probably hasn't changed much since the glaciers carved out the ridges.

The long, rigorous hike is not for beginners, and I was glad I worked my way up to it. But even though it was tiring, I enjoyed the different topography and wild, natural forest.

Before I left, I put on an orange vest, because I was headed into the deep woods. I set out from the parking lot at the southern shore of Beach Pond, off Route 165, a once-popular swimming spot that was closed in 2008 but is still open as a boat landing.

The blue- and yellow-blazed trail in the Arcadia Management Area started just east of the lot and climbed a hill to reach a ridge that leveled off under young and old pine trees. The path skirted an abandoned picnic site built in the 1930s by state and Civilian Conservation Corps workers whose camp was nearby on Escoheag Road. The federal CCC also maintained a recreation area at Beach Pond.

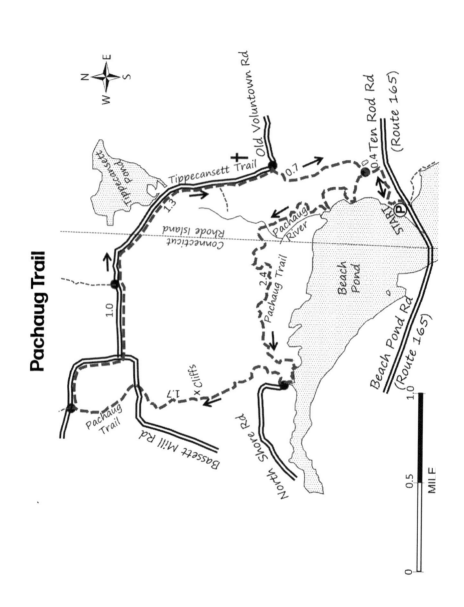

The Pachaug Trail runs along the base of 40-foot cliffs that weep water and are covered with green moss and lichen.

At a fork in the trail, I stayed left on the blue-blazed Pachaug Trail that curled down a long slope to the pond, turned back into the woods and then returned to the rocky shoreline. From a ledge that juts into the water, I paused, felt a chilly wind off the pond from the west and watched a lone kayaker paddling far offshore.

The trail wound back into the woods and through a section of blown-down trees. I rock-hopped over two streams and the Pachaug River, which runs to the pond. Another fast-rushing stream was too wide, though, and I bushwhacked 30 yards upstream to cross.

The trail entered Connecticut. There's a registration mailbox, a side trail to the right if you want to shorten your hike and a sign for entering the 26,477-acre Pachaug Forest, the largest in Connecticut.

The trail then ran west along a series of cliffs, caves, and outcroppings before turning into a short, flat stretch through some private property, with stone walls where somebody once tried to live.

The path curls down to a boat launch at the northern tip of Beach Pond, where kayakers put in for a quiet paddle.

The path crossed a private road and reached a boat launch on the northern shore of Beach Pond before continuing north on the far side of a parking lot. The terrain gets tougher from there. The rocky trail runs along the base of 40-foot cliffs that were weeping water, and then snakes around glacial boulders, up and down ravines and through narrow clefts. I used my hands for balance in several tricky passages.

The trail rises along a ridgeline and then dips under tall hemlocks to a swampy area that seldom sees the sun. The green moss and lichen-covered rocks and ledges were slippery.

I passed another hiker who pointed out some small piles of stones and suggested they were Native American ceremonial spots. Not sure about that.

The terrain eventually flattened, and about 4.5 miles from where I started, the trail exited on a gravel road. The Pachaug Trail goes left and west. I went right, and off the sides of the road I saw caved-in cellar holes, side trails and an abandoned fire lane.

At the Rhode Island line, Connecticut workers placed some boulders

Hikers have to navigate rocky trails that run through deep clefts in glacial boulders.

in the road. But that didn't stop a couple of mountain bikers who roared through.

Just ahead and visible through the trees on the left is the southern tip of a pond named Tippecansett, a Narragansett term for "at the gathering."

The pond and property north of the road is privately owned by the South County Rod & Gun Club. Hikers can hear target shooting in the distance.

The road bends south and joins the yellow-blazed Tippecansett Trail.

On the left, the Firetower Trail runs north to Escoheag Hill. I stayed on the main path that joins Old Voluntown Road.

On the right, a barely-visible white blaze marks a side trail to Wildcat Spring. I took the spur but couldn't find any water bubbling up through the rocks.

Back on the main trail, I had better luck locating a small, gated cemetery on the left with headstones for George Hoxie (died 1854) and Stephen Congdon (died 1902).

The yellow-blazed Tippecansett Trail then breaks off on the right along a path that may have been a fire lane. I walked about a mile under maples, beach, and oak trees until I picked up the joint blue- and yellow-blazed trail that I started out on and followed it back to the parking lot.

In all, I hiked an eight-mile loop on sections of the Pachaug Trail, which runs for 24 miles, and the Tippecansett Trail, which runs 10.5 miles.

That means I still have much more rugged territory to explore.

Trail Tips

What to Wear for Safety and Comfort
- Headgear: brimmed hat, bandana, scarf
- Sunglasses and sunscreen of SPF 30 or higher
- Gloves
- Shirt: lightweight, synthetic fiber, long sleeves, layers to take off as weather warms
- Pants: long pants with pockets
- Socks: wool or synthetic
- Footwear: boots, athletic shoes with sturdy sole and tread, good ankle support

What to Take
- First-aid kit: adhesive and elastic bandages, moleskin, gauze, insect repellent, antibiotic, antiseptic wipe, Antihistamine, ice pack
- Map, compass
- Cellphone
- Two liters of water, in refillable bottles
- Pocket knife or multi-purpose tool
- Extra clothing: socks, windbreaker, rain gear with hood
- Food: protein bar, trail mix, dried fruit, nuts, peanut butter

For Longer Hikes
- Matches and firestarters
- Whistle
- Flashlight or headlamp, extra batteries
- Shelter: plastic tube tent or plastic trash bag or bivy sack

Preventing Tick Bites
- Avoid tick-infested areas, such as tall grass, by walking in the center of trails.
- Tuck pant legs into socks so ticks can't get inside.
- Wear light-colored clothing.
- Cover as much of your skin as possible.

- Put on repellent, especially around ankles, wrists and exposed skin.
- After a hike, inspect ankles, behind knees, under arms, in and around ears, and in and around hair.
- Check boots, socks and clothing to avoid bringing ticks into the house.

Reading Trail Blazes

Many public trails are marked with rectangular blazes painted on trees.

Because public preserves often have many trails, each path is blazed with a different color.

The blazes are placed just above eye level so the hiker, while walking, can glance up and pick up the trail.

There is no universal standard for blazing trails, but the photo of this key shows the most common markings.

Continue straight	Start of trail	Right turn
▮	▮▮	▮ ▮
Spur leading to a different trail	**End of trail**	**Left turn**
▮ ▮	▮▮ ▮	▮ ▮

Requirements for Wearing Orange

All users of Rhode Island management areas or undeveloped state parks are required to wear solid, Day-Glo fluorescent orange such as a vest or hat during deer, small game, archery, turkey and other hunting seasons.

For example, a minimum of 200 square inches of orange is required

Trail Tips

What to Wear for Safety and Comfort
- Headgear: brimmed hat, bandana, scarf
- Sunglasses and sunscreen of SPF 30 or higher
- Gloves
- Shirt: lightweight, synthetic fiber, long sleeves, layers to take off as weather warms
- Pants: long pants with pockets
- Socks: wool or synthetic
- Footwear: boots, athletic shoes with sturdy sole and tread, good ankle support

What to Take
- First-aid kit: adhesive and elastic bandages, moleskin, gauze, insect repellent, antibiotic, antiseptic wipe, Antihistamine, ice pack
- Map, compass
- Cellphone
- Two liters of water, in refillable bottles
- Pocket knife or multi-purpose tool
- Extra clothing: socks, windbreaker, rain gear with hood
- Food: protein bar, trail mix, dried fruit, nuts, peanut butter

For Longer Hikes
- Matches and firestarters
- Whistle
- Flashlight or headlamp, extra batteries
- Shelter: plastic tube tent or plastic trash bag or bivy sack

Preventing Tick Bites
- Avoid tick-infested areas, such as tall grass, by walking in the center of trails.
- Tuck pant legs into socks so ticks can't get inside.
- Wear light-colored clothing.
- Cover as much of your skin as possible.

- Put on repellent, especially around ankles, wrists and exposed skin.
- After a hike, inspect ankles, behind knees, under arms, in and around ears, and in and around hair.
- Check boots, socks and clothing to avoid bringing ticks into the house.

Reading Trail Blazes

Many public trails are marked with rectangular blazes painted on trees.

Because public preserves often have many trails, each path is blazed with a different color.

The blazes are placed just above eye level so the hiker, while walking, can glance up and pick up the trail.

There is no universal standard for blazing trails, but the photo of this key shows the most common markings.

Continue straight	Start of trail	Right turn
▮	▮▮	▮▮
Spur leading to a different trail	**End of trail**	**Left turn**
▮▮	▮▮	▮▮

Requirements for Wearing Orange

All users of Rhode Island management areas or undeveloped state parks are required to wear solid, Day-Glo fluorescent orange such as a vest or hat during deer, small game, archery, turkey and other hunting seasons.

For example, a minimum of 200 square inches of orange is required from the second Saturday in September until the last day of February and from the third Saturday in April until May 31.

During shotgun deer season in December, 500 square inches is required. Violators are subject to a $100 fine.

For more information about the state's hunting seasons and the requirements for wearing orange, go to https://dem.ri.gov/orange.

Wearing orange during various times of the year also is required at many public preserves managed by non-profit organizations. Check the organizations' web sites and signs posted at the trailheads for the requirements.

Trail Conditions

Trail conditions change quickly in different seasons and can be icy, snow-covered, frozen, flooded, muddy, wet or bone dry. Also, blow-downs of trees after storms may block paths.

Many organizations have websites with contact information, either by email or by phone, to check trail conditions. Some preserves have trail stewards or custodians who live onsite and can offer details about what shape the trails are in.

Also, hikers often post online reports of what they encounter. If you can't find a report from just before your hike, go back to a report from the same time last year for some idea of what the trails may look like.

Group Hikes

An experienced hiker should lead. No one should pass the leader, who should stop to regather the group at trail splits, water crossings or obstacles.

Share information with hikers traveling the other way about anything unusual about the trail.

Spread out to keep from eating each other's dust and to decrease the impact on the environment, but remain within eye and ear contact.

An experienced hiker, called a sweeper, should take up the rear. Nobody should fall behind the sweeper.

Trail Etiquette

Stay on the marked trails to prevent erosion and damage to vegetation and wildlife habitat.

When hikers approach from the opposite direction, stop on the side of the trail and let them pass.

Hikers going uphill have the right of way because generally they have a smaller field of vision than those going downhill.

If you are passing a hiker from behind, a simple "hello" or "on the left" is the best way to signal your presence.

More "Walking Rhode Island" Columns

Additional hiking columns by John Kostrzewa appeared on these dates in the Sunday Providence Journal.

2021

February	7	Grills Preserve, Westerly	*Easy to Moderate*
	21	Lawton Farm, Scituate	*Easy*
	28	Sakonnet Greenway, Middletown	*Easy*
March	14	Fort Wildlife Refuge, North Smithfield	*Easy*
	21	DuVal Trail, South Kingstown	*Easy to Moderate*
	28	Burlingame North, Charlestown	*Moderate*
April	25	Osamequin Nature Preserve, Barrington	*Easy*
	25	Great Swamp Fight Massacre Monument, South Kingstown	*Easy*
May	16	Durfee Hill Management Area, Glocester	*Moderate*
	30	Green Fall Pond, Hopkinton to Voluntown, Ct.	*Moderate*
June	6	The Berkshires	*Easy*
	13	Blackall/Ballou Preserve, Cumberland	*Easy*
August	8	Sprague Farm Town Forest, Glocester	*Easy to Moderate*
	22	Powder Mill Ledges Wildlife Refuge, Smithfield	*Easy to Moderate*
September	5	Emilie Rueker Preserve, Tiverton	*Easy*
	12	Roaring Brook/Browning Mill Pond, Exeter	*Moderate*
	19	James Turner Reservoir, East Providence	*Easy*
October	3	Nicholas Farm Conservation Area, Coventry	*Moderate*
	17	Big River Management Area, West Greenwich	*Moderate*
	24	Beaudoin Conservation Area, Coventry	*Easy to Moderate*
	31	Five Ocean Hikes	
November	6	Deep Pond, Exeter	*Moderate*
	20	Touisset Marsh Wildlife Refuge, Warren	*Easy*
	28	Queen River Preserve, Exeter	*Easy*

December	5	Mowry Conservation Area, Smithfield	Easy to Moderate
	12	My Five Favorite Hikes	
	19	Thoreau Walk, Providence	Easy

2022

January	9	Pocasset Ridge Conservation Area, Tiverton	Easy to Moderate
	16	Hemlock Ledges, Exeter	Moderate
	23	Carr Pond, West Greenwich	Easy to Moderate
	30	Hikes in Florida	
February	20	Lincoln Woods State Park, Lincoln	Easy
	27	Rome Point, North Kingstown	Easy
March	20	Canonchet Preserve, Hopkinton	Moderate
	27	Trestle Trail, Coventry	Easy
April	3	Peck Pond/Pulaski Park, Glocester	Easy
May	1	Steere Hill Farm Conservation Area, Glocester	Easy to Moderate
	8	Calf Pasture Nature Area, North Kingstown	Easy
	15	Wahaneeta/Woody Hill Management Area, Westerly	Easy to Moderate
June	12	Curran State Park, Cranston	Easy
	26	Lime Rock Preserve, Lincoln	Easy to Moderate
July	24	Crawley Preserve, Richmond	Easy to Moderate
	31	Connors Farm Conservation Area, Smithfield	Moderate
August	7	Beaver River, Richmond	Moderate
	21	John C. Whitehead Preserve, Dundery Brook, Little Compton	Easy
	28	Diamond Hill, Cumberland	Moderate
September	4	Brushy Brook, Exeter	Moderate
	11	King Preserve, North Kingstown	Easy
	18	Basket Swamp Preserve, Tiverton	Easy
	25	Arcadia East	Moderate to Difficult
October	9	Camp Shepard, Smithfield	Easy
	16	Quonochontaug Barrier Beach, Westerly	Easy

November	13	Black Hut State Management Preserve, Burrillville	*Easy to Moderate*
	20	Mercy Woods, Cumberland	*Easy to Moderate*

2023

February	5	Tucker Woods Preserve, Charlestown	*Easy*
March	11	Browning Woods Farm, South Kingstown	*Easy to Moderate*
	18	Tippecansett South Trail, Hopkinton	*Moderate to Difficult*
April	2	Exeter Historic Cemeteries, Exeter	*Easy to Moderate*
	16	Blue Pond, Hopkinton	*Easy to Moderate*
	30	Canonchet Farm, Narragansett	*Easy*
May	14	Mill Pond, Charlestown	*Easy to Moderate*
	28	deCoppet Estate, Richmond	*Easy to Moderate*
June	11	Town Pond and Oakland Forest, Portsmouth	*Easy*
	25	Grills Wildlife Sanctuary, Hopkinton	*Easy to Moderate*
July	9	Sammy C. Trail/North Camp, Charlestown	*Moderate*
	23	George Washington Management Area, Burrillville	*Moderate*

How to Find the Columns

Copies of the Sunday Providence Journal are available in most libraries. The "Walking Rhode Island" columns are inside the Rhode Islander section of the paper.

If you are a Providence Journal subscriber:

Go to www.providencejournal.com

On the homepage, click on the magnifying glass search icon on the top of the page.

If the icon is not there, click on the three parallel lines in the left hand corner of the screen and the search function should pop up.

Type in Kostrzewa.

The headlines of all the "Walking Rhode Island" columns will pop up.

If you don't have a Providence Journal subscription:
  Go to www.facebook.com
  Search for my name—Kostrzewa.
  All the columns are posted on Kostrzewa's Facebook page.

Or use a search engine, such as Google, and enter the name Kostrzewa and the trail/place you want to hike.